For more information or to book a live event visit our website at

https://evenifmemoir.com/booking

Cover Design By HADIYAH BOBBITT

Interior Design By HADIYAH BOBBITT

ISBN 13: 978-1-7376241-3-4 Paperback

ISBN 13: 978-1-7376241-9-6 Hardcover

First Edition

www.evenifmemoir.com

EVEN IF

A MEMOIR IN VERSE

EVEN IF

A MEMOIR IN VERSE

FAITH IS THE WEAPON OF WARFARE

HADIYAH BOBBITT

SENSITIVE CONTENT DISCLAIMER

This book addresses violence, suicide, and events that may be considered sensitive or emotionally disturbing. This material may not be suitable for all ages.

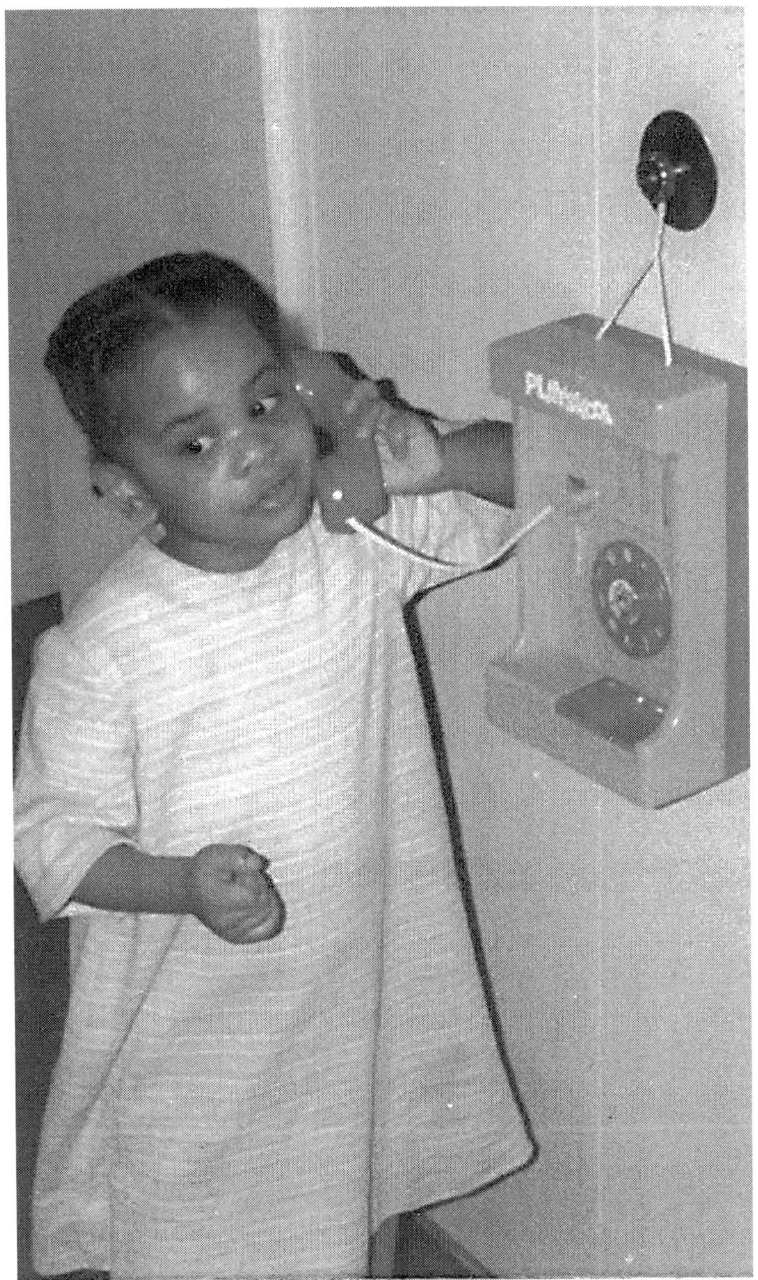

DEDICATION

A bird without wings cannot fly.
How will she survive?
A child cries. No one hears.
Who will dry her tears?

For Mooshie

EPIGRAPH

Because he lives I can face tomorrow
Because he lives all fear is gone
Because I know he holds the future
And life is worth the living just because he lives
And then one day
We'll all cross that river
And fight life's final war with pain
And then, as death gives way to victory
I'll see the lights of glory and I'll know he reigns

William J. Gaither, Gloria Gaither.
Because He Lives.

CONTENTS

EVEN IF…

EVEN IF SOCIETAL VALUES SHIFT, EVEN IF CULTURAL NORMS ARE COMPLETELY OVERTURNED, EVEN IF AN ENTIRE POPULATION BELIEVES OTHERWISE, GOD'S PRINCIPLES CANNOT BE ALTERED. HIS LAWS ARE AS OLD AS TIME ITSELF. HIS TRUTHS NEVER CHANGE.

– DR. A.R. BERNARD

FOUR THINGS WOMEN WANT FROM A MAN

PREFACE

This collection of poetry and prose reflects a turbulent journey that arrives at an irrevocable trust in God. The title is a declaration of faith chosen at the beginning of one of the most challenging periods of my adult life – the fight against COVID-19. As of this writing, more than four million people have died as a result of the illness. By the grace of God, I survived.

After a prolonged case of COVID-19, the battle continued. Unfamiliar to many is the torrent of post-COVID syndrome or post-COVID conditions. It can present with complications and a constellation of symptoms as diverse as the individuals themselves. For some, it is mild or short-term. For others, it is persistent and debilitating. It is a shadow of sickness and uncertainty for all.

I extend my deepest condolences to everyone who has lost family and friends to COVID-19. Your loss is devastating, and your heartache is unimaginable. I pray the peace of God comforts all who have suffered from the illness or experienced it with sick loved ones. May God bless you richly with the incomparable peace of His presence.

Curating this body of work has been transformative. The vision for Even If began as a collection of work that inspires faith, encouragement, and perseverance through life's struggles. The journey reaches a place of empowerment and authority obtained only after walking through fire and exiting with unparalleled refinement. The poems lay bare the remnants of abuse, neglect, depression, death, and the suicide of my sister – the most devastating event of my adult life. Bringing the vision to realization during my COVID-19 and post-COVID battles underscored strength in dependence on God is the only way to victory. My journey has been one with seemingly endless adversity. Yet, overcoming with faith-filled perseverance and resilience is an eventual guarantee.

Selecting poems written several years ago, looking at them with fresh eyes, and combining them with new work, was unexpectedly healing. This book dedicated to my late sister includes pieces about her suicide and my experience of her absence. I polished older pieces and gave more color to her story. Writing about her life and reflecting on the path that led to her suicide drained me emotionally and mentally. I spent a great deal of time refining stories about her, choking back sobs when thinking of past events that were too brutal to put on paper. Somehow I managed to overlook a profound truth. I was looking at my own story—from the same tree with the same root. But she and I were very different fruit. Our stories were not identical, but they were dreadfully close.

There is a crucial distinction in our paths. Even when I had no hope left to hold onto, I was convinced hopelessness was unacceptable. The song "Because He Lives." could be the soundtrack to seasons I weathered wearily.

> Because he lives, I can face tomorrow
> Because I know He holds the future
> And life is worth the living just because he lives.

In the most challenging seasons, simply knowing there is a God who created heaven and earth and all therein—including me—gave me hope. Although at times, facing tomorrow was face down in a tear-soaked pillow, immobile and crushed by the weight of grief, it was tomorrow nonetheless, and I made it there. No matter how small it may seem, that was a win. I was 24 hours closer to the other side of the situation. Simply knowing He's there, He can see me. And He can do anything, so something's going to have to change. Knowing it could only be Him, I thought it would be disrespectful to make requests in prayer and not be still and wait for a response. Being restless in God's waiting room is better than writhing out in the cold, fearful, and faithless.

I collected the old and new stories of our dreams, fears, and nightmares. I found our lives, and her death provides evidence that faith in God can change everything.

This collection became more than a poetic journey of spiritual growth, victory after a labored crawl through darkness, drowning in suffering and grief. It is more than a testimony of discovery, revelations from the furnace of afflictions, perfecting in God's refining fire, and the illumination of the beauty borne from ashes.

A sense of urgency rose as I thought of the people who feel the same way my sister felt when she took her life. I think of the people who feel they have reached their end – suffering in silence right now– isolated from others for their lack of understanding. It breaks my heart, and I wish I could do something or be there to comfort them.

I pray this book brings solace and encouragement in knowing that someone understands the lowest lows and has been down there yet rose in strength. I pray that you find hope and inspiration in knowing there may be times of suffering, but they will not remain forever. There is sustaining peace, strength, and endurance when reaching for God. Religious acts, ceremonies, eloquent prayers, or quoting scripture are not required to reach God. I prayed one, two, and three-word prayers when I didn't know where to begin. "Jesus." “Help." "I need you." "Please, Lord." "Come get me." "I don’t know." "Please." God is not doing a word count on your prayers. He does see, hear, and capture each tear from His children. One silent tear can be a prayer louder than a cry bottled inside. He hears all. Answers or changes may not be immediate. I rarely see answers or change immediately. But, his spirit is a comforter, enabling stillness to receive His peace while waiting in faith.

YOU GET A CLOSER LOOK AT THE FEET OF JESUS
IN SUFFERING THAN YOU DO IN SUCCESS.

– CHANDLER MOORE

SOCIAL DALLAS

INTRODUCTION

The Gift

New York City is often called the greatest city in the world. Being a "New Yorker" is a significant part of the identity of some. While I consider myself a New Yorker, it is part of my experience, not my identity. As we begin our journey together, I will share a more intimate view of who I am. To put it plainly, I am a gift from God—sent from heaven.

Contrary to what my sister would have said in response, this is not arrogance or a delusion of grandeur. In the Arabic language, Hadiyah actually means "gift." So, there. I am glad we have that out of the way.

I have made failed attempts to pass myself off as an acceptable gift during holidays and birthdays by wearing ribbons and bows. It was cute once, but it got old quickly. Candidly, I think I was the only person who found it funny. The best jokes are often the ones most amusing in your own mind—that is where all the fun happens. My name also translates as "Guide to Righteousness." We will get to the guide and righteousness part later.

I was not planned; many of us were not – no heartbreak there. I can sensibly remove the rose-colored lens and accept that I was not conceived intentionally; at least, it was not my parents' plan. So I can also say unequivocally, although they did not send for me, I am sent. God was emphatic about my presence here.

> *"God saw all that he had made, and it was very good." Genesis 1:31*

We can conclude my initial premise is accurate. I am a heaven-sent gift from God.

Grab a highlighter or pen because the following lines you read are some of the most meaningful truths in this book. I encourage you to write them down. You are a gift from God, heaven-sent. God unequivocally issued the mandate that you be present in the world at this very moment. Per Genesis 1:31, as referenced above, that is a good thing. Everything God creates is done well. Especially you. So we are almost like twins. I feel like I know you already.

If you know anyone from Brooklyn, New York, it is likely one of the first few things you learn about them. I have heard it ranked with the same importance as; I'm engaged, newly married, pregnant, went to Harvard, or from Brooklyn. As of the writing of this, I am not engaged, newly married, or pregnant. College and grad school were both in New York. You have probably guessed by now the most important of the five. I am from Brooklyn – born and raised.

I will always consider Clinton Hill in Brooklyn, New York, my hometown. With its blocks lined with beautiful historic brownstones, trees more than 100 years old, a 10-minute drive to Manhattan, a 15-minute walk to the city view from the Brooklyn Bridge, and nearly everything you could want nearby 24 hours a day. There is no place like it. I add the qualifier of being born and raised in Brooklyn to underscore the importance and clarify one point. On occasion, I met people who, when asked about their origins, say Brooklyn. If the hair tingles on my arm, I can't resist asking what part and for how long. It breaks my heart to bear the bad news to these kind and beautiful people. They mistakenly think moving to Brooklyn 10-15 years ago or purchasing property in

Brooklyn makes them "from" Brooklyn. I say this with the warmest regards; you are not "from" Brooklyn. You live here. If this misconception has duped you, I forgive you, and yes, we can still be twinsies. We will need each other on this journey.

THE GUIDE

Having the name that means Guide to Righteousness has always felt like a heavy mantle to carry, especially with having the "Yah" of "Yahweh" in my name. In the past, in immaturity, I told people that if they are looking for a guide to righteousness, they should follow me under no circumstances. Today, I am honored, humbled, and in complete submission to my spiritual and human identity rooted in our God Yahweh. So if you are looking for a guide to righteousness, please follow me. There are two reasons why I openly extend the invitation. First, I wake every day with the desire to walk a path of righteousness. Second, and equally important, we will undoubtedly fall along the way and need someone to help us stand. I hope you're still on board with the twinsie thing. We don't have to dress alike. We can just wear the same cool shades or something like that.

> *God created man in his own image, in the image of God created he him; male and female created he them. Genesis 1:27*

THE SCRIBE

Creativity is on the list of desirable traits shared across all sides of my family. Writing; poetry, prose, and generally speaking flowery has been a natural inclination. I have been accused of being dramatic, I'd say charismatic. My sister often said it is like watching a performance when I share events or experiences. As written in Shakespeare's "*As You Like It*," I believe, "All the world's a stage, And all the men and women merely players." I was born this way; deal with it. I have a cadre of appreciators. Though their number may be just enough to use an HOV lane, and one may require a certificate of rabies vaccination for air travel, to them, I take a bow.

Inspiration comes randomly; driving, in the shower, and even in the middle of a conversation. Other times one word or a lyric in a song can trigger a spoken word piece that is phenomenal—complete fire. There are stacks of scarcely filled journals, torn envelopes, and crumpled paper with random scribbling going back quite a few years. There are pieces I don't recall writing, things I shared on social media more than ten years ago, undated quatrains on old laptops, notebooks, and obsolete mobile devices. What comes like a flash in the pan inspiration captured on paper or some other device, though clever or heartfelt, is sometimes forgotten as fast as a sneeze. Nevertheless, scrawls on wrinkled half sheets of paper, faded boarding passes, or an upcycled store receipt in a bag in the back of the closet echo whispers from within. They are the hidden history of feelings given figure internally but muted by external noise.

My earliest memory of writing poetry was at the age of seven. This poem was about an orphan. I imagine the poem could not have been long, but I likened my life experience, all seven years, to that of an orphan. My only reference for life as an orphan would have been an over-dramatization in a movie or on television. It must have depicted a sad child, alone and abandoned. I don't recall the words, but they were not well received. After reading it, there was a heavy silence. My parents were not pleased. Frankly, they were probably offended. They were married, and at that time, we all lived under the same roof. I expect it is offensive for one's seven-year-old child to write a poem about feeling like an orphan. This was an unplanned veiled declaration "You are failing at your job."

I am amazed at seven years old; I had the emotional intelligence and reflective ability to write a poem about how dismal I experience life. In essence, I penned the first of numerous cries for help. I can only be grateful to have had an outlet for extreme emotions at such an early age. Unfortunately, in my early years, the only place my sentiments were heard was on paper. The intensity of emotion was captured by the depth of each mark on the page, the place tears were allowed to speak, where each word was heard, even if I had no understanding. Paper was the podium. The outpour was often revelatory.

I sometimes wonder what I am going to learn about myself whenever I have the unction to write. When unclear on feelings stewing inside pencil gave it a voice and paper gave it a stage. Outwardly, comedy concealed tragedy. Internally, somber brokenness and confusion laced with rage demanded an audience. Eventually, I ran out of paper.

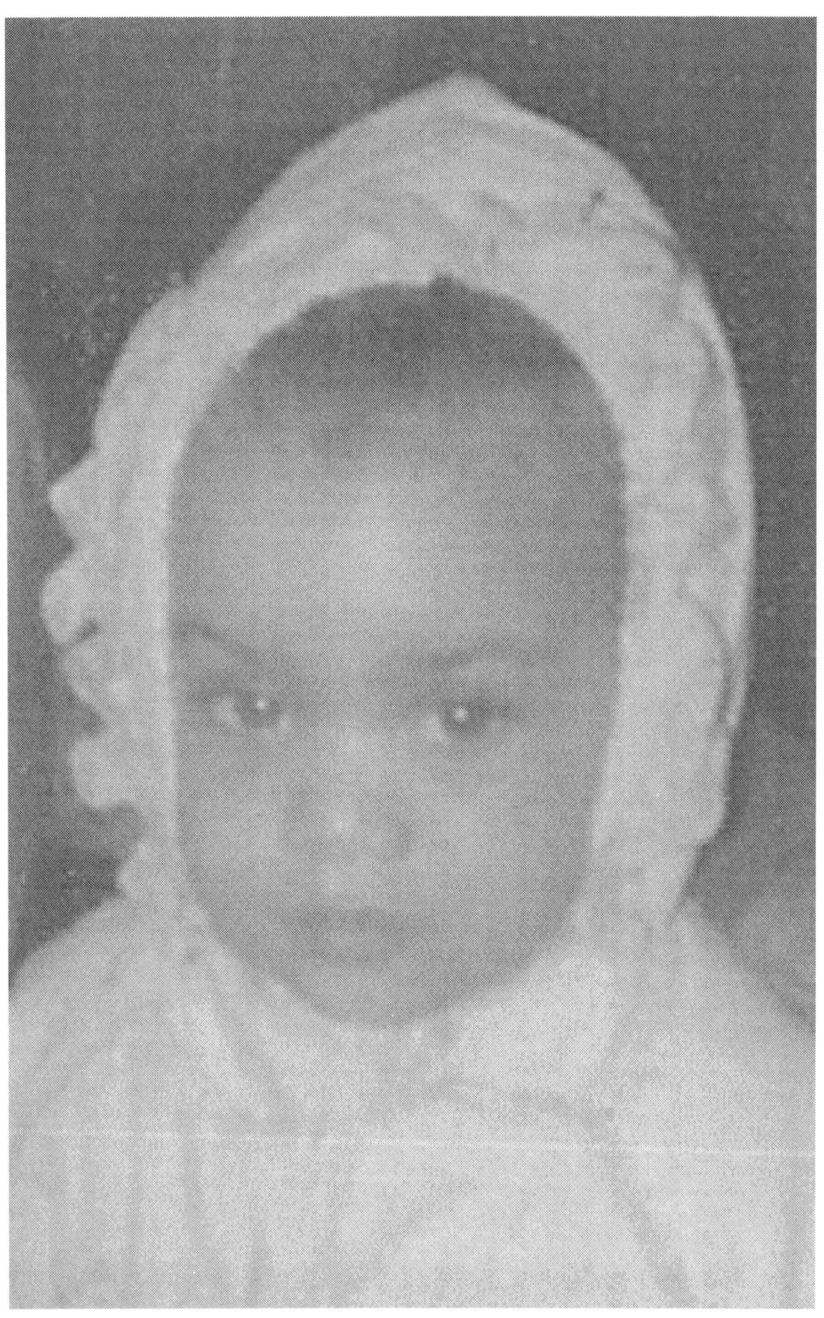

ACCORDING TO YOUR FAITH BE IT UNTO YOU.

MATTHEW 9:29 KJV

EVEN IF

I made a declaration of faith on May 9, 2020. I put the words "Even If" on paper and hung them in a mirror to be seen daily. In the middle of a personal COVID-19 battle, I stood with a conviction. Even if the darkness of the current pandemic covers the earth and the thick darkness of sickness over people across the world, the current troubles in my life are nothing when I think of the great things in the future.

Even as I suffered, I could not forget the countless times I received blessings and favor so great that it baffled those around me. Some periods seemed like I walked on sunshine and was carried by the clouds. There have been unexplainable, seemingly impossible, miraculous blessings in my life so great no one understood.

There have also been unspeakable tragedies and adversity that seemed impossible to endure or survive. There were experiences, so horrid witnesses were unable to understand how I made it through at all.

My conviction is this; God is still the same God He was yesterday, today, and forever.

Even If was initially inspired by stalwart faith demonstrated by Shadrach, Meshach, and Abednego in the third chapter of the Book of Daniel. Even under the threat of death in a blazing furnace, they refused to worship any God but their own.

> *"The God we serve is able to deliver us from it, and he will deliver us... But even if he does not, we want you to know,*

> *that we will not serve your gods or worship the image of gold you have set up." Daniel 3:17-18 NIV*

Even if COVID-19 hit me, I still praised God for who He is. Even if things do not look good, I'm going to pray until they do. Even if fear starts to creep in, I know it's hard to worry while worshiping—so turn the music up. Even if I'm too weary of formulating a prayer, there is still a Psalm and song that magnifies God in every situation. Even If became a posture of faith, even in suffering.

> *For I cried out to him for help, praising him as I spoke. Psalm 66:17 NLT*

EVEN IF is the signature on the masterpiece that is my life, anchored in Isaiah 43:2;

> *When you walk through the fire of oppression, you will not be burned up; the flames will not consume you. Isaiah 43:2 NLT*

EVEN IF is a suit of armor, a shield of faith in Elohei Ma'uzzi, God who is my strong fortress. 2 Samuel 22:33

EVEN IF is the platform built on a principle. I am made in the image of God, who has declared He will be Chomah Esh, a wall of fire around his children and its glory within. Zechariah 2:5

EVEN IF is a banner that proclaims the God who is Esh Oklah, the all-consuming fire, created me in His image and for His glory. Deuteronomy 4:24

EVEN IF declares; I don't fear the fire of adversity. I am fire.

EVEN IF holds Stand Your Ground authority in the face of adversity living by castle doctrine. As a child of God, wherever I stand is God's sovereign territory—everything against me is ultimately powerless.

> *"You are from God and have overcome them, for he who is in you is greater than he who is in the world." 1 John 4:4 ESV*

EVEN IF is a stamp that nullifies incoming memories and reminders that seem like postcards from hell.

You can begin to understand a person's purpose by observing where and how they were designed and refined. You gain further insight by how they enter and exit the trials, tribulations, and miserable conditions imposed upon them.

While thinking about challenges—there were plenty—I reflected on my life and past experiences. There is a pattern woven through my history. I win. Even if I have tripped, stumbled, or fallen, I win. Even if I lost all, failed, grieved with the most profound depression, suffered full on assaults on my mind, body, and soul throughout my life, I still win. Despite all that has happened, I can look back and laugh even if it occurs again. I've already won.

There are no battles without bruises or soldiers without scars. Every victor has had to be vicious and face hostility. There is no war hero without war wounds. I was born a warrior.

Even if my entire world comes crashing down, my identity is unchanged. Endurance increased my base strength. Everything ever taken or withheld is worthless, all meaningless compared to the blessings of God and the certainty of my future. The situation is insignificant. The God I serve is greater than all. I was made in his image, therefore, designed to thrive – not just stay alive. Survival is situational—resilience is a lifestyle.

DEAR FRIENDS, DO NOT BE SURPRISED AT THE FIERY ORDEAL THAT HAS COME ON YOU TO TEST YOU, AS THOUGH SOMETHING STRANGE WERE HAPPENING TO YOU.

1 PETER 4:12

OPEN BOOK TESTS

My faith walk began 20 years ago. One year, I developed an exceptional thirst for the word of God. During that period, my appetite was insatiable. Beyond Bible studies and devotional time, the voice of God and the word of God was the only thing I wanted to hear. Even on the go, I listened to the word all the time. I played the audio Bible in the car while driving, throughout my house during the day, and let it play low in the background when I went to sleep. I have routines programmed on my smart devices to open the bible skill and play the scriptures that are part of my daily meditation.

It was a beautiful period. I was operating in new spiritual gifts. I woke each day excited to see what new thing the Lord was going to do that day. I later learned that unusual thirst was a clear indication the Holy Spirit is moving in you mightily. And it is in preparation for a significant life-changing season ahead. So it is no surprise that I was at the height of this unquenchable thirst for the presence of God and constant immersion in the word in 2019.

Let's pause for a minute. Imagine moving through 2019 carried on a cloud, in a manner of speaking. Things that would have kept me up at night or reminded me of the part of myself that is not entirely transformed—the "I'm saved, but I'm still from Brooklyn" side that needs sanctification—had no effect. My only explanation is that the Lord anesthetized me from adverse people and situations during that period. There were the normalities of life, but I forgot annoyances as quickly as they came. I know I was being covered in a new way. I was set apart for that season and basked in God's presence as if nuzzled in a heaven-sent incubator. 2020 pulled the plug.

You never know what's on the inside of a sponge until you squeeze it. Everything in it will drip all over the thing squeezing it. If it's empty, you have nothing. I believe we are spiritual sponges. Adversity is the big rough grubby hand that squeezes us when we are spring fresh and neatly perched in our lives. Because we know there will be adversity, affliction, and long-suffering, we have to stay ready. As the saying goes, you don't have to get ready if you stay ready. Enter 2020.

On a mild Wednesday evening in February 2020, a few weeks before the pandemic slammed the US and shut down New York City, I felt a little extra spunky. I squeezed in a session with my personal trainer before choir rehearsal. Then, just as we were wrapping up cardio on the treadmill, I turned to step off and somehow managed to fall and sprain my ankle. I literally limped into the big rough grubby hand of the pandemic of 2020. By March, the whole world went limp.

We often hear the saying, "Let go and let God," "God will make a way," and the often-misquoted Romans 8:28, "God works all things for the good." 2020 was a year to put your faith where your mouth is—not money. When you are home alone sick from COVID-19 with lungs filled with fluid, a fever of 104, an oxygen level below 90%, and imminent inflammation on the brain—no bank account, stack of cash, or black card can help you. Faith creates an atmosphere for miracles; it was my sustenance, it has no price tag, but it was tested.

Three months after rebounding from COVID-19, sudden post-COVID complications hit me like a freight train. I was home alone and suffering. At that time, post-COVID conditions were not widely understood, even among the medical community. The intensity and random nature of the onslaught of symptoms were daunting. I felt helpless. At times tears were my only prayer and only praise.

Yet, even in my worst state, what I thought was the lowest point, I said to God, "I know you see me. I know you hear me." I asked, "Is this what we're doing? Is this going to be the thorn in my side?" In a pit of despair, he's still there with me.

> *And be sure of this: I am with you always, even to the end of the age. Matthew 28:20 NLT*

My spiritual family prayed fervently throughout this time. Staying connected with people who have the same convictions is necessary. Faithless, doubters, and nay-sayers should not be stirring your pot. I stayed connected with those who are in complete agreement in faith and prayers.

> *A person standing alone can be attacked and defeated, but two can stand back-to-back and conquer. Three are even better, for a triple-braided cord is not easily broken. Ecclesiastes 4:12 NLT*

The teacher is silent when you are taking a test. I was sure I was in the furnace of affliction, and testing was in progress. It is a thirsty place where faith is the only answer to this kind of test. The best tests in primary school were the open book tests. Tests of faith are just that, open Bible tests. So when you find yourself in the furnace, you better have a well of answers to draw from and the ability to find the answers quickly. My well was the word of God and His promises.

If you get your life from Me and My Words live in you, ask whatever you want. It will be done for you. John 15:7 NLV

A “Daddy, you said…” prayer is the pillar when I don’t have a leg to stand. Answers aren’t always immediate, but I trust and wait. When I thought I was at the lowest point in my post-COVID syndrome battle, the symptoms were physically and emotionally debilitating. It felt like I lived in a bottomless pit of despair, falling in deeper every day. Those who I may have been able to lean on in the past seemed to vanish.

But God gives us assigned sisters, appointed to walk alongside us on our journeys. He gave me Andrea and Tamesha. My beloved beautiful spiritual “sister-queens,” as we call each other, gave me shoulders to lean on and selflessly carried me on my worst days. They brought the lifesaver of joy when I was up to my neck in a sea of despondency that I wasn’t able to articulate. My girls inspire, nurture, and pray down fire from heaven. They are women of God who carried me in the spirit when I couldn’t walk or crawl—serious prayer warriors. I love my sisters, especially when they tolerate my quirks and love me anyway. One day while I was in the eye of the storm, we were on a prayer call when Tamesha made a prophetic declaration, “She cannot write what she has not lived.” She reminded me of my purpose. This is all part of the plan; preparation to serve God in the life He designed. I am confident God is the best designer – better than I’ll ever be.

There are people we don’t know depending on us to pull through hard times. We are all here to carry each other. We cannot lead someone through paths we have not navigated and mastered well enough to bring others to light and safety. There are people we have yet to meet—like YOU!—waiting to hear what we have suffered, survived, and the spoils of the war gained from enduring to the end. I reaffirmed I would be the last woman standing.

Post-COVID fog is smothering. It can render you incapable of finding clear thoughts, let alone words worthy of prayer. In my spirit, I knew that I could not wake up to a banquet of blessings every day and only give God a saltine-cracker prayer. My spirit refused to submit to my state of mind and emotion. On days like that, a "psalm and a song" is how I hold on.

One night a song came to mind with persistence as if nudging me to listen to it, similar to a song being stuck in your head with no relief until you play it. The challenge was that I hadn't heard the song in a long time; I didn't recall the name, who sang it, or where I heard it last. I remembered the lyrics said something to the effect of even rocks praise God. That was enough for me to think rocks were not going to upstage me when I'm born with a voice of generations and the very breath of God in my lungs. I was half asleep, in the dark with my phone Googling fragments of lyrics and searching YouTube for the song. I recall the lyrics referred to Luke 19:40.

> *Some of the Pharisees in the crowd said to Jesus, "Teacher, rebuke your disciples!" "I tell you," he replied, "if they keep quiet, the stones will cry out."*

Let us pause for a brief digression. Imagine being in a crowd with Jesus, along with his disciples and others, joyfully praising the Lord. The Pharisees wanted to silence their praise and asked Jesus to do so. Jesus said, "if they keep quiet, the stones will cry out." The response is His deity, His sovereignty, His identity. He did not respond to the situation, why His disciples should continue to praise, or why the Pharisees are wrong. Essentially, He declared I am God. His response to the circumstance is who He is, just as written in the old testament scripture.

> *"Everything on earth will worship you; they will sing your praises, shouting your name in glorious songs." Psalm 66:4 NLT*

It will be a great disservice to you if I do not digress a smidge more. One question for your consideration; what would your life look like if you responded to every situation declaring who God is related to the situation?

In sickness, He is Jehovah Rophe, Healer. In lack, He is Jehovah Jireh, Provider. When fearful, He is Jehovah Elohim Tsaba, our God of Hosts, commanding armies of angels to encamp around us. Anxious or worried? He is Jehovah Shalom, our Peace. Lost? Need direction or guidance? He is Jehovah Roi, our Shepard. Overwhelmed by uncertainty, He is Jehovah Sal'I, lean on the Rock of ages. In all things, He is Immanuel, God with us. Nothing can stand against Him.

I encourage you to reflect on this regularly. Feel free to fashion those truths into a crown and wear it with royal authority—by activating them. Put them in the empty spaces when life has you puzzled. Let's continue.

The idea of rocks crying out to God louder than me was unacceptable. Music is vital in my life, so nothing is going to steal my song. It was time for a new fight song. In college, I listened to various types of music while studying. But there was only one song for prepping on the day of a test. Study music varied, usually Jazz or Classical anything from Brubeck to Bach. However, on the day of a test, from quizzes to finals, there was only one song; M.O.P.'s "Ante Up Remix." The remix—an important distinction—was my fight song, an academic "knuckle-up." Clearly, my taste in music in college was not sanctified—keeping this 100—but my GPA was. A redeeming factor, perhaps? My taste has changed significantly since then.

After foraging through YouTube for what felt like an eternity, I found the song, the artist, and a new video with a performance that was next level. *So Will I (100 Billion X)* by Cross Worship featuring Osby Berry was uplifting. I played it for days. I am grateful for that incessant midnight nudge. It ultimately led me to Maverick City Music, a new source for a new fight song. Lord knows I needed them.

Regardless of your state of mind, you cannot listen to a Maverick City Music playlist and stay in the same spirit. It will bless you; you will be amped and there will be a shift in the atmosphere. You will likely feel like you went to a praise and worship service and, at some point, be on your feet or in your chair dancing. If this does not happen, please have someone check you for a pulse.

Pandemic ordinances have the doors of most churches shut. So we adjusted to online services and have our private praise parties in pajamas while choir robes sit crisp and unworn. MCM has dominated the playlist in my house regularly.

A bigger bonus is that they led me to the gospel artist whose voice became my foreground and background music for months and even now – Chandler Moore. His album *Feelings* spoke to how I felt throughout 2020 and 2021. The lyrics resound precisely how I felt during what seemed like a post-COVID syndrome prison as if someone read my journal and put a track on it. The timing of the album release could not have been better. Thank you. Thank you. Thank you.

YouTube seems to have loads of videos of Chandler ministering throughout the US and abroad. His unbridled passion and transparency in authentic worship are a godsend. Sometimes, you never know how much your work, art, or words benefit the lives of others. A shortlist of people and things carried me through this tumultuous period, his work is counted among them. I extend gratitude to the people who contributed those videos, especially those responsible for the 3-hour montage. I could hug you.

Honoring the Lord by surrendering your gifts, operating in your calling, and doing the things for which you were anointed is golden—the best and only way to a great life. I pray the Lord rewards you all and your families 1,000-fold. Blessings to you all.

On days I was too exhausted to leave the bed, I played worship music and read Psalms. Some songs became big fuzzy warm blankets. Instead of monotonous brain fog babbling, my morning prayer began with reciting Psalm 51. Later, I incorporated Psalm 91, 25, 77, and 119 into a daily recitation as I physically and spiritually got back on my feet, with half-decent clarity and more intentional prayer life. I let my over-imaginative creative tendency, which often takes on a life unto itself, lead the operation. I created scripture cards with beautiful images and fonts and set them where I rested most frequently. One of my idiosyncratic ways of staying weapons ready, sword at hand.

> *"Put on salvation as your helmet, and take the sword of the Spirit, which is the word of God." "For the word of God is alive and powerful. It is sharper than the sharpest two-edged sword, cutting between soul and spirit, between joint and marrow. It exposes our innermost thoughts and desires." Ephesians 6:17, Hebrews 4:12 NLT*

Throughout 2020 and 2021, I was in a vice grip of adversity, enduring things that would have sent some off the deep end. While weathering COVID-19, post-COVID events, and a monsoon of maladies, a firm foundation of faith and a stronghold on the scriptures anchored me. I have lived enough to know, trust, and believe;

> *"They that wait upon the Lord shall renew their strength; they shall mount up with wings as eagles; they shall run, and not be weary; and they shall walk, and not faint." Isaiah 40:31 KJV*

Life's circumstances will test your faith, mainly through suffering, especially after bold declarations and big wins. I made my Even If declaration at the start of my COVID-19 battle and constant irritants have put it to the test. There were long waits in dark and dismal waiting rooms—the mental and emotional space during that period. These were times I could not walk or run. Crawling was an accomplishment.

I am still waiting for God to move in areas of life. Waiting on God to act is not a one-time event or situational. It is a way of life rooted in unconditional trust in Him. In every situation, when I can't, He can. Even when I can, He can do better. Some consider God a last resort. He is my first choice—and the only answer to the tests.

Testing is performed to prove if something is functioning as designed or programmed and uncover areas needing refinement. Testing is conducted to determine one's aptitude in a particular discipline. Tests also evaluate fitness for elevation to a higher level. Sometimes I think, “I did not register for this class!” But I can guarantee I will do more than pass. I’ll be taking names and kicking…

TOGETHER THEY WILL GO TO WAR AGAINST THE LAMB, BUT THE LAMB WILL DEFEAT THEM BECAUSE HE IS LORD OF ALL LORDS AND KING OF ALL KINGS. AND HIS CALLED AND CHOSEN AND FAITHFUL ONES WILL BE WITH HIM."

REVELATION 17:14 NLT

THE ART OF WAR

A skilled artisan knows the precise formula, method, environment, and conditions required for the perfect expression of their craft.

In ancient times, warriors were chosen at birth. Newborn babies were evaluated physically to determine if they would grow into men who could withstand combat. Those chosen to become warriors began training at age seven.

The training methods used in preparation for their lifelong service were merciless, dangerous, and extreme. When they reached the age of 12, training intensified, preparing them to be unstoppable, fight fearlessly and without end. They were deprived of resources, subjected to sleep deprivation, exposure to the elements, living in the wilderness with little more than a light cloak in hot and cold climates. In-fighting was encouraged. Shaming and heckling were commonplace. They had to forage or steal if they wanted more food than the tiny bit apportioned.

Endurance was tested regularly by being beaten and flogged, even to the point of death. We would consider their training physical and psychological savagery—or 2nd Grade in my life but that's my scandal—I digress. They believed this training course used the methods, environment, and conditions necessary to produce warriors needed for the battles ahead. Fighting fearlessly until death was expected and considered duty fulfilled.

The pattern of this preparation process is painfully familiar. The chosen are chosen—not just chosen for war, but predestined warriors appointed to win.

In Christ we were chosen to be God's people. God had already chosen us to be his people, because that is what he wanted. And God is the One who makes everything agree with what he decides and wants. Ephesians 1:11 ICB

As sure as there is day, there is night. As sure as there is darkness, there is light. So when you have an absence of peace, be ready to fight —and always ready to defend your body, soul, and mind. What some would call bootcamp I call life. To call 2020 and 2021 a period of war would be an understatement. But, I think it has also been a training ground.

In the book of Ephesians, the apostle Paul gives insight into what is happening in the unseen realm.

Put on the full armor of God, so that you can take your stand against the devil's schemes. For our struggle is not against flesh and blood, but against the rulers, against the authorities, against the powers of this dark world and against the spiritual forces of evil in the heavenly realms. Ephesians 6:12 NIV

What is this armor he speaks of? I am glad you asked. In his second letter to the church in Corinth, he writes:

For though we live in the world, we do not wage war as the world does. The weapons we fight with are not the weapons of the world. On the contrary, they have divine power to demolish strongholds. 2 Corinthians 10:3-4 NIV

Paul gives us our formula, the methods, environment, and weapons necessary to win the war against the evil one.

Therefore put on the full armor of God, so that when the day of evil comes, you may be able to stand your ground, and after you have done everything, to stand. Stand firm then,

1. *Stand firm then, with the belt of truth buckled around your waist*
2. *Stand firm then with the breastplate of righteousness in place*
3. *Stand firm then with your feet fitted with the readiness that comes from the gospel of peace. In addition to all this;*
4. *Take up the shield of faith, with which you can extinguish all the flaming arrows of the evil one.*
5. *Take up the helmet of salvation*
6. *Take up the sword of the Spirit, which is the word of God.*
7. *Pray in the Spirit on all occasions with all kinds of prayers and requests.*

With this in mind, be alert and always keep on praying for all the Lord's people. Ephesians 6:13-18 NIV

There are quite a few in-depth teachings on The Armor of God. Priscilla Shirer's teachings are among my favorites. As is the fruit of her ministry, her teaching on The Armor of God is thorough and empowering to put it mildly—you will be battle-ready. She is a mighty woman of God, and her teaching of the Word of God is powerful, fervent, and transformational. When I need a refresher but do not have time to sit and read, her books on Audible and YouTube videos are my go-to.

The Full Armor of God is incomplete without all seven parts—obviously. When one is missing or weak, there is a severe vulnerability. I am not establishing an order of importance. However, you are in serious trouble without prayer and the word of God. The shield of faith has been top of mind. Not only does it extinguish "all" the flaming arrows of the evil one, but it is everything. I love when God gives us an “All.” Faith holds it all together. It takes faith to hold the word of God as truth, to trust we have been endowed with righteousness, peace, and salvation. Faith in the Lord our God is the bedrock.

If there was anything I could hold on to during this marathon of tests, trials, and the spiritual wars waged against us all, it was faith that God is who He is. Some days I have to remind myself, it does not matter how I feel. It does not matter what things look like, and it does not matter if everyone’s thoughts or opinions differ. God did not wake up with me this morning and decide to operate according to my feelings, fleeting circumstance, or others opinions. As my Pastor, Dr. A.R. Bernard, says, God is not schizophrenic.

Faith draws on the power of God, and its power never ceases to amaze me. Even though I wait with expectation, I still marvel at how God operates. Primarily when I think of the years when I lost faith or had none at all. The very concept that our faith in God is a catalyst of His infinite power is mind-blowing.

As I would explain to my five-year-old Godson, there is something inside you; the ability to believe in God and His ability. You can learn of God's ability and choose to accept it as truth. In so doing, you can ignite God's infinite power. I do not pretend to understand. As my Pastor asks, “How can a finite mind comprehend the infinite?”

In Mark 5:24-34, there is a woman with issues of excessive bleeding. She exhausted all her resources, yet no doctor was able to heal her. One day she heard Jesus was near walking with his disciples along with a large crowd. She believed just touching his garment would heal her. So she went out to where the crowd gathered around Him, crawled on the ground reaching for him. This woman was willing to go to great lengths to get to Jesus. Would you crawl on the ground to get to Jesus? She reached Him and touched His garment. She was healed in the physical realm immediately.

It is worth noting this scripture says after the woman touched him, "At once Jesus realized that power had gone out from him." In a crowd of people, if someone touched the bottom of your draping cloak, would you feel it or sense it at all? He said to her;

> *"Daughter, your faith has healed you. Go in peace and be freed from your suffering." Mark 5:34 NIV*

Before she touched him, she had the conviction that He could heal her. She decided to act on that conviction. The belief that He is who He says He is, drew on his power. Her faith healed her. That faith developed before she saw him and before she touched him. Her faith healed her before she got down and crawled to him. What she decided in her mind and fixed in her spirit created healing in the invisible realm. Her action in accord with her faith brought it into the physical realm.

We do not know if she planned to seek him out that morning, moments after she heard He was passing by, or the instant she first heard of Him and His ability to heal. We do not know how long she waited after believing Jesus could and would heal her. The scripture says she suffered for twelve years with constant bleeding, and her faith in Jesus' ability was the fix.

There is no requisite processing time for answers to prayer or the promises that come with faith. Her experience puts a spotlight on the scripture;

> *"Now faith brings our hopes into reality and becomes the foundation needed to acquire the things we long for. It is all*

> *the evidence required to prove what is still unseen." Hebrews 11:1 TPT*

Though days can be dark and stormy, we trust all storms pass, and the sun will rise again and even shine brightly. It always has; we believe it always will. Likewise, life circumstances can feel like endless stormy nights of hurricanes, monsoons, or typhoons—I think I have had them all simultaneously. Nevertheless, there will be morning, and there will be sun, and there will be joy. While it may not be tomorrow or next week, the storms will pass, the sun will rise again, and even shine brightly. Of course, things may break in the storm; relationships, dreams, your current source of sustenance, and what may seem like your life as you know it. But God can put things back together better than you can imagine. Especially if you think the broken thing is you. I have been there. I can say with certainty, what I thought broken was being made better—most notably me.

I will be praying for you, that your faith increases and becomes your anchor, as Jesus has already prayed for us. We will endure and rise victorious, even if it feels like the wait is endless. Faith is the dominant factor in waiting. As I wrote in Praise v. Pain, worship wages war on worry. So I press through—and at times merely hanging on—in faith with prayer and with faithful prayer warriors and praising God for who He is. Because He is who He is, as written in His word, He does what He does. No one does anything as well as He does. The best is worth the wait.

Waiting is a strategic and tactical response to uncertainty. It demonstrates an understanding that you have no idea greater than God's plan. It is a preemptive strike against the enemy's plot to reposition you outside the will of God—a dangerous place.

THEY FOLLOWED HIM RIGHT INTO THE HOUSE WHERE JESUS WAS STAYING. SO JESUS ASKED THEM, "DO YOU BELIEVE THAT I HAVE THE POWER TO RESTORE SIGHT TO YOUR EYES?" THEY REPLIED, "YES LORD, WE BELIEVE!" THEN JESUS PUT HIS HANDS OVER THEIR EYES AND SAID, "YOU WILL HAVE WHAT YOUR FAITH EXPECTS!" AND INSTANTLY THEIR EYES OPENED—THEY COULD SEE!

MATTHEW 9:28-30 TPT

ALWAYS WRITE

Journaling was a part of recuperating from post-COVID conditions. Gradually, I returned to writing for pleasure. During this period, the poems and spoken-word pieces seemed to flow freely, pouring out naturally. They range from anguished lamentations, unashamed transparent testimony, and full-armor battle-ready faith declarations.

More than one year after my initial Even If declaration, more than a year of challenges put it to the test. When those challenges rang me like a sponge, what came out was all I absorbed in the preceding period. Satiating a constant thirst for the presence and word of God throughout 2019 filled the storehouse in my heart. My recent work is laced with what poured out while I was under pressure. It is the word of God, my fortress and foundation of faith. There are poems of prayer, cries for help, moments of doubt, self-affirmation, and a return to walking in God-given power—His strength made perfect in my weakness, despite the circumstances. Some lyrics are based on the truth and promises in the word. These pieces have scriptures that align with the lyrics. You can find them in the Biblical Scripture Reference section at the end of this book.

When you read something you would like to locate in the Bible or read the poems with the applicable scripture, the text of the verse(s) and versions are listed for your convenience. You are welcome.

We all have ideas about God and what God thinks of us. We make choices based on these ideas consciously or unconsciously. If they are contrary to scripture, the life you build with your choices will be founded on false information. You can't build your best life without the best information. In the same way, I can confidently go to God in prayer requesting His written promises with, "Lord you said in your word...." and expect a "Yes, my precious beloved daughter, it is my good pleasure to endow you with all good things, according to your faith, it is yours."

His words measure my choices, actions, and inaction; His principles for living, how He instructs, how He chastens, and what He approves and rewards. I sometimes imagine getting an "Atta girl.", "Is that what I said?", "Well done my good and faithful servant.", "That is not how we do things.", "Let's take that up a notch.", "Be still. I am God. Period. Sit down while I work" And a, "Lo, I am with you always. Even to the end of the age." "I love you, and nothing can take it away."

A thought life grounded in the knowledge and truth of the incomparable privilege and beauty of being a child of the God of all heaven and earth, the almighty, all-knowing, all-seeing, all-powerful, and all-loving, results in living in and with royal authority. You can wear a crown with confidence when you know indubitably your father is the King.

Hearing or reading inspirational material is excellent. However, the power is in your personal grasp of the word of God and your relationship with him. So, as you read these poems, I pray the words reach your heart and reveal God in a new way.

> *"The Word became flesh and dwelt among us, and we have seen his glory, glory as of the only Son from the Father, full of grace and truth." John 1:14 ESV*

Learning from teaching and preaching is only part of the process of spiritual growth. The core is having the word written in your heart directly from the Bible.

> *"Study this Book of Instruction continually. Meditate on it day and night so you will be sure to obey everything written in it. Only then will you prosper and succeed in all you do."*
> *Joshua 1:8 NLT*

I invite you to read the foundational truths of personal authority, power, resilience, and all you have been designed to be and have. Then, consider the scripture reference sections highlights of your benefits package and a few rules of the road. We are already on the job and the clock.

The word of God is life. When Jesus responded to adversaries, He did so with the scriptures. The word of God is sharper than a double-edged sword. I pray this work leads you to add more of the word of God to your arsenal of faith so that you can speak it over every circumstance.

Some of the poems written later in the journey captured within this book can only be describe as divinely inspired. As I wrote, I received them as messages of hope, reminders of who I hold onto in faith. Sometimes, the most meaningful encouragement comes from within, and it must be disseminated. I believe the Lord is using this work to present Himself through His Word in a new way, through a unique perspective and experiences that may resonate with someone in a way like no other.

I hope you encounter nuggets of wisdom to cherish; bricks to throw at monsters that haunt; bombs to drop when the devil taunts; gems for your crown; God's word written on your heart; a sensitivity to the hand of God on days you can't lift a finger; and insight and encouragement to share with the souls that will cross your path. I pray that our journey brings healing, hope, and an arsenal of faith in the knowledge of God. Faith is a weapon of warfare. Stay armed.

A MAN CANNOT PLEASE GOD UNLESS HE HAS FAITH. ANYONE WHO COMES TO GOD MUST BELIEVE THAT HE IS. THAT ONE MUST ALSO KNOW THAT GOD GIVES WHAT IS PROMISED TO THE ONE WHO KEEPS ON LOOKING FOR HIM.

HEBREWS 11:6 NLV

HOME

There was a long morning in her journey.
There was a long journey that morning.
There was long mourning in her journey.
At times the walk was all alone.
Thank God she made it home.

EVEN IF I WALK THROUGH THE VALLEY OF THE SHADOW OF DEATH, I WILL NOT BE AFRAID OF ANYTHING, BECAUSE YOU ARE WITH ME.

PSALM 23:4 NLV

THE WRONG PATH TO PEACE

Tajh was my elder sister and only sibling. Born in Brooklyn, New York, during the winter of 1975 to a couple married after a brief six-month courtship. Her birth name was Tajma. Her friends called her Tajh. She was peculiar, playful, with a bizarre sense of humor, and a heart more delicate than choux pastry. Unfortunately, she also loathed my existence from the day I was brought home from the hospital. I was not part of her plan either.

Complications during my birth raised questions of if and when I would make my New York City debut. It was a long journey. It seems I caused a bit of a kerfuffle as I made my entrance. I try not to make that a habit. To my friends and family, please forgive me, I was born this way. When I arrived, doctors decided respite in the hospital's neonatal intensive care unit would be best. A few days in the exclusive accommodations of their finest incubator had me camera-ready.

When she first laid eyes on me, Tajh immediately demanded I be thrown in the incinerator. Apparently, I was invading her territory. The story was told with levity over the years. I did not find a word of it funny—not ever. In retrospect, is it not odd that a child younger than five demanded the execution by incineration of her newborn baby sister. It seems I was born into a war with enemies in wait.

Eventually, she grew to tolerate me and even assisted in my effort to begin walking. I believe she planned to train me up to be her servant. She was woefully mistaken. Tajh always had big ideas.

Some were good, others not so much—like her aforementioned execution by incineration initiative proposed days after my birth. Some of her ideas were brilliant, brilliantly destructive, and sometimes dangerous. I could write an entire book titled "Dumb Stuff My Sister Did." Her response book would have been titled "Brilliant Ideas My Sister Ruined." Trust that I am not attempting to paint myself as a saint. While I was quite proficient at putting on the face of an angel—a saint, I was not. If nothing else, we were a creative clan.

There was one endeavor she attempted too many times. She failed all, except the last. In her teens and her 20s, she tried, half-heartedly. Finally, in her 30s, she followed through. In North Carolina, on the night of Thursday, October 25, 2007, my sister, my only sibling, committed suicide by shooting herself in the head.

Life can seem unreal – but nothing more real than death. The responsibility of handling her final affairs fell to me. I flew to North Carolina, where she lived. It was evening when I arrived at the police station in Raleigh. I insisted the detective take me to the site where she left us. She was in a car parked beside a large tree large enough to cover the entire vehicle. I wondered if she noticed it. She used to talk to animals and plants playfully. I ponder mildly humorous nonsense at the most inopportune times—a temporary escape from the painful reality.

Years before her death, she asked me how I can live a "normal" life after the hell we endured in our formative years. I wonder what she considered "normal" and how she could possibly see it in me. I told her it was Jesus, the peace of God that transcends all. Life was not walking on a cloud day by day, but in the center of it all, it was and is the Lord that keeps me and has kept me from completely falling apart when life seems to unravel. She immediately retorted with an ignorant condescending diatribe on how weak I must be to turn to Christianity.

Then, somewhere down the road, she was invited to a bible study by someone she respected. She eventually came to know Christ. Sometime later, she called me with a childlike wonder and enthusiasm to know she received Christ. It is comforting to know where and with whom she rests.

As I stood in the center of her death, I wondered if she forgot about the Lord. Did she talk to God? He hears our cries and sees our tears before we are aware of them ourselves. Did the storm in her mind get so dark? Was it so dismal she could not think of another way to run to his arms? I guess she forgot you can always find Jesus on your knees if you get down on them, call on him, and be still. I wondered if she remembered how often I said, "I wish I were an only child."

What was her last thought as she pressed cold metal against her head? I can see her crying. I can picture the anguish on her face. I recall how her face sunk in sadness. Her cries were always full of despair. Wordless wails that scream, "Why doesn't anyone see this pain. Why won't anyone make it stop." I have seen it hundreds of times. It is the unseen pain that darkens the spirit and stains the soul deepest.

Were there demons of despair that tormented her with reminders of her mother's physical, mental, and emotional abuse during the first ten years of her life? How many operatives of evil replayed decades of angst; reminders of neglect; being battered by her mother, rejected and discarded by her father, betrayed by friends, shunned by me when she attempted to be the bullying big sister, tormented, beaten, and bullied by the world. I wondered how frequently she recalled being violently gang-raped at 14. Those memories don't fade.

Tragedy leaves the deepest wounds. Hers were innumerable. Triumphs were trumped by torment; all was tainted by torture. She saw no sun nor hope for tomorrow, just nightmares in her mourning, faded dreams of joy overshadowed by sorrow.

Did she forget I told her it's a pain she wants to escape, not life itself? Did she call me as she did in the past? She called midweek early one morning. It was an odd time for her call. She was in North Carolina, sitting in her storage space with a gun in her hand. She told me what weighed her down so heavily, the circumstances she found herself in. It is rarely the situation at issue. Instead, it is the operating system, the method of thinking to handle that circumstance, or the lack thereof.

I stayed on the phone with her. I asked her to get help; she said that she would. I think. I asked her about the medicine she was prescribed in the past. She said it made her feels strange. Does death feel strange? Hers feels strange to me. I do not recall how long we stayed on the phone, but I know I almost did not make it to work that day. We talked through the situations, and when she finally felt settled, she decided to put the gun away and move forward. The next day she called to apologize for scaring me and said she is the older sister. She should be the one looking after me. That was a rare occurrence.

Not too long after that call, I went to Florida to get away from New York for the weekend. As my flight landed, I saw a missed call and voicemail from a relative I rarely speak with. Immediately I knew

I was facing one of two situations. My father is dead, or my sister committed suicide.

I listened to the message. Before words, the tone of voice confirmed it. My sister is gone. I sat on nearby steps. I asked out loud, "Why did you do it?" The answer came to mind immediately. It is wretched to have an instant understanding of a siblings' suicide. It came from the all too keen awareness of the impact of the visceral history we shared. Her life was a nightmare, and she couldn't wake up. I know it well enough to understand why death seemed to be the only source of peace. It is disturbing to understand someone's suicide.

There was a sea of questions, opinions, and expectations of understanding. Discussion with others was unnecessary. I did not have the energy nor desire to explain the kind of pain that could cause someone not to want to wake again. Their ignorance cannot invalidate anguish they would not be able to understand. God has all the answers. I welcomed them to get them from him. I am sure I tastelessly used expletives while making the suggestions.

At the end of that day, there were three things that I knew unequivocally. First, my sister is finally free from pain. Second, more importantly, she is singing with angels and elders at the throne of the Lord—no better place. Third, at the end of all, I am an only child.

LET THE LORD WATCH OVER US WHILE WE ARE SEPARATED ABSENT FROM EACH OTHER REMEMBER THAT GOD IS OUR WITNESS EVEN IF NO ONE ELSE IS AROUND US. HE WILL KNOW IF YOU HARM ABUSE MY DAUGHTERS

GENESIS 31:49-51 EXB

HELP IS AVAILABLE

If you or anyone you know is thinking of or has decided to commit suicide or has expressed the idea of suicide. Please connect with one of the resources listed immediately.

CALL

Emergency number 911 (US and Canada) 999 (UK)

National Suicide Prevention Lifeline 1-800-273-8255

The Lifeline provides 24/7, free and confidential support including Spanish-speakers and anyone who is deaf or hard of hearing.

Suicidepreventionlifeline.org

ONLINE CHAT https://suicidepreventionlifeline.org/chat/

TEXT

Crisis Text Line -- Text Hello to 741741 fields messages about suicidal thoughts, abuse, sexual assault, depression, anxiety, bullying, and more. You can text 741741 in the US or UK (686868 in Canada)

YOUTHLINE

Text teen2teen to 839863, or call 1-877-968-8491

MONSTERS

Death begins inside
Publicly, they say, "Smile."
Outside,
tears are something the civilized hide.

What happens when inside
is the only place to cry?
Hidden here, no one sees.
A soul's slow death begins inside.

You can't hide suicide.
It lurks behind the eyes
Eyes hindered cries

The heart still secretes
poison hidden deep.
Secrets secrete toxins that dissipate
life in an endless search for peace.

There are no secrets between scars
just untold stories
battles
no glory.

Flags flew half-mast
on poles, hearts were hung on.
Someone said, "Be strong."
She was barely holding on.
Already too long.

It looked like something was just off, – Just wrong
The nightmares don't end
when the monsters are gone.

"EVEN IF AN ARMY GATHERS AGAINST ME, MY HEART WILL NOT BE AFRAID. EVEN IF WAR RISES AGAINST ME, I WILL BE SURE OF YOU."

PSALM 27:3 NLV

HOW LONG?

He said, "Hold on." To what, and for how long?
I grasped at empty air; even my lungs couldn't find
not even a breath to cry out for help
just empty, unheard, hollow yelps.

"Just hold on. I need you to be strong."
Words too often said.
"I need you to be my strength,"
said the small voice in my little head.

I wondered what life would be like,
if I were better off dead.

Sticks and stones,
no worse than bricks thrown at home.
He said I am not alone.
But this place can't be called a home.

Will someone come, rescue me?
I can't stay here.
I can't play here.
There is nothing I can say here.

But "be strong." He said.
He needed me to hold on.
To what,
and for how long?

There is a new dawn, so I've heard
where there is no cage for a songbird
but a stage for her to sing on
in a place she's actually heard.

Was it in a book I read somewhere,
or something someone told me?
Was it a vision, something out of a dream
or my mind where I created things to believe?

In there were the things I held onto.
The external, unreal, and unreliable reality,
run from it was the best thing to do.

One day I might be still.
Someday I may grow strong.
Someday that little voice will get loud,
and proudly say, "you've got it wrong."

"I should not be the strong one.
That's not my job to do.
My meekness magnifies your weakness.
I should be holding onto you."

I did hold on to the bit of hope
I crafted inside my head
shaped by words whispered,
“There’s something greater up ahead.”

IF YOU WILL LOOK FOR GOD AND PRAY TO THE ALL-POWERFUL, IF YOU ARE PURE AND RIGHT AND GOOD, FOR SURE HE WILL HELP YOU. BECAUSE YOU ARE RIGHT AND GOOD HE WILL PUT YOU BACK WHERE YOU SHOULD BE. AND EVEN IF YOUR BEGINNING WAS SMALL, YOUR END WILL BE VERY GREAT.

JOB 8:5-7 NLV

DROWN

I sometimes need a hand when I forget to hold on
and can't find what to hold onto
when my feet can't find good ground
and I don't have a leg to stand on.
What's wrong?

Do you see me here adrift?
All directions missed
each tear a smoke signal
wondering where I am
where you are

Where are you? Can you hear me? Here?
Sobs are songs, not sad ones, not blues,
just the only way I can say I need you.
Help.

Something broke this boat.
It's capsized; I'm drowning.
Can you see, the sea, rivers of fear,
blood in the water, the nightmares?
Sharks surround
memories flying overhead are
vultures pushing me down
under water. Will you let me drown?

I'm calling up to where I need to be.
Can you hear me? Here?
Sometimes I need a hand.
Could you lift me, carry me?
I forgot what to hold on to.
My feet can't find good ground.
Please don't let me drown.

EVEN IF I AM INNOCENT, I CANNOT LIFT MY HEAD, FOR I AM FULL OF SHAME AND DROWNED IN MY AFFLICTION.

JOB 10:15 NIV

DO OVER

Do you need to make me over
or remake me?
Please remake me
or just take me
from me. Save me.
I wronged all my rights
I heard you still forgave me.
—Thank you.

You take me from places
where I should have never been.
Sin—fails—no wins.
Take me for a do over.
Can we begin again?
Can you be my friend?

When I reached my end
I saw you endlessly
never-ending nonstop
loving me.
Can we begin again?
Will you be my friend
so I can see?
Please show me.
Only you know me.
Show me the way you see me
only you can show me.

Hold me.
You know the feeling of a fall.
Hold me
so I can let go of it all.
You are my one phone call.

Call me by my true name,
the one only you know.
I'll come running.
Don't let me fall.

Your call is the only answer.
Your words guide my feet
—when I hit walls
your light shines down on me.
Lift me above; you are my all
save me; I am yours.
Yours is the only name I can call.
Jesus, Take my call.
Call me by the name only you know.

Save me.
Your arms—the only place I can go.
I am blinded make me see
only what you can show.

Tell me
can we begin again?
I think you are my only friend.
Really all I need at the end of it all.
You are my all—Jesus
—the only name I call.
Take my call.

EVEN IF WE ARE FAITHLESS, HE WILL STILL BE FULL OF FAITH, FOR HE NEVER WAVERS IN HIS FAITHFULNESS TO US!

2 TIMOTHY 2:13 TPT

LOST AND FOUND

When good things happened
I thought you were around.
When bad happened
you were nowhere to be found.

I thought what I had, was all I could see.
Here on the ground,
Lord, can you see me?
Here, in Lost and Found?

I sing along with the songs
that you'd never let me down.
But you left, and I can't see anything,
laying here on the ground
in Lost and Found.

Can you see the cries I cry?
I leave them in a jar at night.
I heard the songs where you dry tears.
Is your wonderful work done in darkness?
Show me tonight.

At night—No pen—no light
it's dark in Lost and Found.
Memories sting, thoughts tormenting
gone—I still hear the sound.

I sang the songs they sing
that you show up every time.
This time you must be off the clock,
not the shift when you seek and find.

Everyone and everything
is broken all around
including me—long forgotten
here left in Lost and Found.

Why do they call it Lost and Found?
It should be called Lost.
Most that are left, long forgotten
things no one wants just left behind
rotting.

It makes sense now
to think I never did belong.
Everything I seem to do was wrong.
I was broken early on

before I had my parts assembled
pristine, was never a day for me
No rightness.
If I am wrong, show me
rightness could ever be for me.

If I am wrong
show me
what found life looks like.
Does it look like me?

I heard them say you are the only one,
who heals the broken hearted.
What do you do with trash like me,
broken from the time I started?

"Damaged" that's the label
they attached to me.
I think.
It is hard to tell
when tossed aside without a wink.

So I lay here in Lost and Found,
way back, in a dark place, sleep.
There's no unfounded hope—lingering,
that someone might come for me.

I do close my eyes, dream.
In them, go places I've never been,
See the things I have only heard of,
places I'll never be.

I heard the song; you go to find The Lost.
Am I the one from your 99 sheep?
Maybe I have wandered off, not really lost
will you come and look for me?

I'll be waiting. I don't know the way
or if there is a way back.
I just thought I'd look up and ask
if you know where I am at.

I hear you know everything.
Does that mean me?
I guess if everything is everything
in here, around the broken and lost,
you still see.

Do you see me?
Should I get ready?
Should I expect you at the door?
Can my friends in here come to?
I think they, too, need something more.

I think I'll step out.
I hear this thing called faith,
is something that activates you.
With a bit—you'll show your face.

I am here in Lost and Found.
In here, there's plenty of the thing called faith.
I'll run and grab some for those who lost theirs.
I heard even for them, you still wait.

It turns out there's so much faith placed here,
down here in Lost and Found.
I wonder if those who have lost it
are also waiting to be found.

I wonder if they, too, are lost
just not in here like us
broken labeled lost
on the bottom
bound.

I didn't know if I touched just some
faith would pull me from the ground.
The rest started coming toward me,
like magnets, waiting to be found.

These faith things propped me up.
I heard them whisper "expectation."
I heard the word; memory is blurred.
If it's part of this faith, yes, please, I'll take some.

So it seems I've risen
to the top
of the Lost and Found
Faith has me lifted, well propped.

I grabbed a whole bunch of extra faith
in case your friends need some faith too
I hear them calling my name now,
to be redeemed. Is that you?

I think I know. I know it's you
coming low to find the lost
According to faith, that is what you do.
Can I reimburse you for the cost?

He said, "Walk with me—
That's all you need to do.
I paid it all—
Back at the cross."

YAHWEH RESPONDS… EVEN IF A THERE IS A MOTHER WHO FORGETS HER CHILD, I COULD NEVER, NO NEVER, FORGET YOU. CAN'T YOU SEE? I HAVE CARVED YOUR NAME ON THE PALMS OF MY HANDS!

ISAIAH 49:15 TPT

I'LL WAIT

I read your book,
the part at the end says you dry tears.
I don't see that happening here.
Do I need to wait until the end,
or is it a fantasy you being my best friend?

I know the tears—you didn't put them there.
Broken people—countless years
Remember when things plagued me,
things most people can't stand to hear?

Plagues pass the other things
—I know they won't last.

Back then, I thought you didn't care.
I stopped caring, for
everyone, everything—even me.
I thought you couldn't see
me—or what I came to be
and if you did, you'd be ashamed
of what was left of me

things I would do and say
I'm sorry I acted that way.

I read where it says
you forgive and wipe slates clean.
If anyone needs that,
it's me.

I feel you tell me stories
while sleeping, in dreams.
Things happen,

things I can't believe
like you're saying,
"You know it's me."

I read your book, where it says
eyes haven't seen ears haven't heard
human minds cannot conceive
the things prepared by the Lord of glory
for the ones that love him.
But you loved first.
I hope there's some for me.

It says all of this will pass away,
if we chart the course of the race and stay
that you will be with us now and always
even until the end of days.

If the rest of my race
is like the last few laps
I'll need your strength,
and everything I lack.
Everything, all I have is your word
I trust that you'll come back
and these words, all you put in your book
even without legs, I'll stand on that.

If I have to wait
for dry eyes
delayed endless days
until the time you ordained
designed purpose
despite pain
praise will remain
to promise unchanged
faith, never in vain
I'll be here
waiting in your name.

EVEN IF THE PRINCES AND MY LEADERS CHOOSE TO CRITICIZE ME, I WILL CONTINUE TO SERVE YOU AND WALK IN YOUR PLANS FOR MY LIFE.

PSALM 119:23 TPT

LET IT GO

"Let it go." Those three words left alone are the most annoying bits of advice doled out—ad nauseam. Of course, one must let go of the past to move forward successfully. However, oversimplifying a process that takes a great deal of courage and healing is ineffective, discouraging, and—in my case—infuriating.

What lit fires were when its four-word cousin accompanied those three words—"You have to forgive." What hurts more profoundly was when it came from family members or anyone who knew where I was stuck.

I thought of sending engraved invitations to each of them, offering a pair of my shoes, a time machine, and an itinerary with maps to the significant locations, dates, and times. The occasion would be going back in time to walk a mile in my shoes. The final ceremony would be their return with an account of their experience and reflection on whether they still have the same perspective and advice for me. Most would not make it back. There were a lot of fires throughout the years.

Further injury was felt when I was beaten over the head with:

> *"For if you forgive other people when they sin Against you, your heavenly Father will also forgive you. But if you do not forgive others their sins, your Father will not forgive your sins. Matthew 6:14-15 NIV*

I did not know how to let go. I did not know why I did not know how to let go. Decades passed before I learned how to "Let it go."

During a Tuesday prayer service, our beloved Elder Pointer spoke on forgiveness. To paraphrase, he said you know you have forgiven when you no longer need the person who spoke ill of you to clear your name, or when you no longer desire the person who betrayed you to confess, or no longer desire repayment or compensation from the person who stole your property. As he spoke, I felt like God was saying to me, "What is better than me? What's better than what I have for you?" Inside I thought, "Oh, my God—nothing." Finally, I found the mental mechanics I needed to process forgiving. That one epiphany changed my view of so much. Being able to forgive and freely dismiss past and present offenses is liberating and life changing.

Nothing tangible or intangible, no amendment with words, actions, or things, was more valuable than all I already have. The very thought was preposterous. If someone stole $50 from you and you were given $50 billion, would you care about the thief? Unlikely. I reflected on the simple shift in thinking. It made everything anyone had ever taken from me worthless. I already have all that is greater than everything on earth or in heaven—the love of God.

A flood of songs and scriptures that detail what it means to be a child of God came to mind—being who I am is priceless. I thought of who I am to Him, who He is to me, what He has done, and done on my behalf—there is nothing more powerful. There is no one greater. He is incomparable. My conclusion was uncomplicated and unquestionable. Letting go is easier when you are holding on to something far more significant. I already had all I need. Jesus.

The core of this confidence, this unwavering certainty, is faith. Faith in who God is. This faith does not rest on the foundation of my experience or my understanding of him. Although, that alone is more than enough evidence for me. This certainty rests on Jesus—the foundation of all life. My faith is rooted in a reasoned trust that God is who He says He is in the Bible, his word. The only thing worse than being powerless is being powerful and not knowing. Ignorance of your possession of power does a disservice to yourself and anyone associated with you. Are you a prince or princess living like a pauper because you don't know your father is the King?

Several scriptures put wind in my cape. My favorites are the explicit declarations that "I got the power!"

> *"...Now all glory to God, who is able, through his mighty power at work within us, to accomplish infinitely more than we might ask or think." Ephesians 3:20 NLT*

Grab a highlighter and a pen. It is important to note and highlight five words in that verse, "*power at work within us.*" I highly recommend writing that down somewhere you can see it regularly. Resting in God's power and presence disempowers the past and unfavorable conditions created as a result of it. Empowerment expands by fueling and reinforcing your faith. Doubt can destroy trust and faith in God. Doubt destroys. If there is anything worth doubting, it is your doubts. Jesus said,

> *"...Truly I tell you, if you have faith as small as a mustard seed, you can say to this mountain, 'Move from here to there,' and it will move. Nothing will be impossible for you." Matthew 17:20 NIV*

Even the size of a grain of a mustard seed, faith is more powerful than any thought or thing. Why a mustard seed? It is one of the smallest seeds, less than a 10th of an inch. When a mustard bush has matured, it grows as high as 20 feet—about the height of a two-story building. That, my friend, is a tremendous return on investment. Plant a seed of faith in God in your heart. Not just faith that He exists, but faith in who He is. Let nothing and no one uproot it, and watch what God yields in you, for you, and on your behalf. Fix your mind on faith that God can do anything but fail. Don't forget to doubt your doubts!

While reading this, some might immediately reflect on why they believe faith does not fit them. Perhaps it is because of their past, present circumstances, or an uncertain future. Perhaps it is regret, guilt, shame, and other corrosive thoughts that create an atmosphere contrary to love, life, and freedom. Trust me, I understand. I had a trailer load. When setting an atmosphere that inhibits life and love, you can be sure death and darkness will take root. If a myriad of dubious "buts" and "what ifs" came swooping down, snatching up your seed of faith. I would encourage you to look across history, especially in the Bible, and be encouraged that there is no "but" too big to stop God from being God-loving, forgiving, redeeming, and reconciling his creations to Himself in Christ Jesus.

Throughout the Bible, the scripture describes the lives and deeds of some of the most wretched, undeserving individuals, including murderers, adulterers, thieves, and prostitutes, who God ultimately redeemed and restored when they chose to turn to Him. There is no end to God's patience, transformative and redemptive love. There is no end to God's love. His word says,

> *But if we confess our sins to him, he is faithful and just to forgive us our sins and to cleanse us from all wickedness. 1 John 1:9 NLT*

There was a time when I thought I grew tired of being a "good girl." I recall saying boldly, "I'm taking my halo off." Intentional about plans to act like the prodigal daughter. I hope and pray you do not ever—NEVER—do, say, or even think of doing the same.

> *Hold on to what you have, so that no one will take your crown. Revelation 3:11 NIV*

I was not aware of it then, but those words—the very thought—opens a door to a world you do not want. Speaking a hint of it is an invitation to knocks at your door that you do not want to answer. The journey home for the prodigal child can be an ugly one.

> *"When he came to his senses, he said, 'How many of my father's hired servants have food to spare, and here I am starving to death! I will set out and go back to my father and say to him: Father, I have sinned against heaven and against you. I am no longer worthy to be called your son; make me like one of your hired servants.' So he got up and went to his father." Luke 15:17-20 NIV*

It is not just a parable. Save yourself the trouble. Stay home. Keep your crown on. You never know what you will step in and trample back home with you. But for the grace of God, as the song goes, "I know it was the Blood for me." God loves us so much, eagerly waiting for us to return to him.

> *"But while he was still a long way off, his father saw him and was filled with compassion for him; he ran to his son, threw his arms around him and kissed him." Luke 15:20 NIV*

When looking back I wondered in jest, if my guardian angels were watching from the sidelines, shaking their heads, waiting for me to choose to turn back and walk the path God designed before I took my first breath. In my youth, I was considered the "good girl" in some circles. This gave me a false sense of being on the right side of wrong. I was wrong—very wrong. The truth is this, a puppy in a pack of wolves is still a dog.

By His mercy, I am and always will be the daughter of the Almighty God. So, if you have a big "But" that you believe precludes you from the love of God—I can say with confidence—your "But" is not that big. Certainly not bigger than God.

BUTTERFLIED

Unwritten love songs
play randomly
repeatedly
in mind

A heart, still standing
stands still.
Eyes, wide shut,
hope filled.

Churning and agitated,
gutted by butterflies.
I sigh,
relief unreleased another day.

I caught his eye
whilc sauntcring by.
His breath stopped,
eyes clocked my silhouette,
carefully crafted
individually wrapped with him in mind.

Dressed for the occasion,
my final destination
all day, throughout thc night
I'll be lingering in his mind
until next time.

EVEN IF A MAN'S TROUBLE IS HEAVY UPON HIM. IF NO ONE KNOWS WHAT WILL HAPPEN, WHO CAN TELL HIM WHEN IT WILL HAPPEN?

ECCLESIASTES 8:6-7 NLV

HEART

Love kept secret
wounds the heart of one who keeps it
makes the heart of one who needs it
hardened—only sorrow feeds it.

THE GARDEN AT MIDNIGHT

We met at midnight
in the garden
where yesterday and tomorrow merge.

Remembered we were bad at being good
Had days when we stayed on the right side of wrong
Rewrote the words to the song the world sings

Sang lullabies to a world sleep
Hoped we'd wake them from death
Deaf heard the blind fumbling through the night
to find the fastest way to darkness.

We stayed free of the un-freed
those living ever after 'happily.'
not knowing evils necessity
needing things to eradicate reality.

We soaked up the sun's rays
in the moons shine
exchanged matters we mind
mindful of matters that remain
the same since the dawn of time.
Ever unchanged.

We toed the thin line between love and hate
Found nothing there but space
and fate,
falling like snowflakes into our hands
grainy like dust and times sand
slipping through our fingers
numbering the minutes hours days.

We met at midnight, in the garden
Rode the back of winds
Wrestled clouds into water streams
Dined on rainbows while drinking sunshine

In the garden
we found that hope is the only thing that grows.
Everything is nothing, and nothing is everything,
no one seems to know.

At midnight, in the garden,
hope sprouts and dreams bloom.
Shadows fade
giving way to a sunlit moon.

Yesterday always was and never is.
Tomorrow is a hypothetical possibility.
When we meet at midnight in the garden
our certainty is now
and you and me.

UNTITLED

Words
like daggers
pierce bleeding hearts
tears never cried
drain
flowing wordless wails
echo through an empty shell
into deafening silence.
Hope discarded
wretched
distressed
strewn wilted flowers
in forgotten graves
on roads no longer traveled
where the dead are the only ones with peace

IT WAS GOOD FOR ME TO BE AFFLICTED SO THAT I MIGHT LEARN YOUR DECREES.

THE PUNISHMENT YOU BROUGHT ME THROUGH WAS THE BEST THING THAT COULD HAVE HAPPENED TO ME, FOR IT TAUGHT ME YOUR WAYS.

PSALM 119:71 NIV, TPT

GOODNIGHT

Songs say what seeps thru tear ducts.
Tears—emotion just gets stuck there.

Let the music love
unconditionally understanding me,
never underhandedly
without need
for me to be anything
—but me.
And that's enough.

In sweats and a tee
make up free
hidden
from what used to be.

In music, I lose it
in a place that understands
when I stand with weakened stature
limp languished lost
damned
I fly, drift aimlessly
on melodies, composed for me.
For right now
I need to be—just me
unconditional authenticity
even if not phenomenally.

Just tonight
would you mind if I disappear
while fingers drift and linger on keys
escaping thoughts of where fingers used to be?

Can I hide
in a Hathaway place and time,
where flawed figures are bad math
but still loveable—because it's mine.

If you don't mind
I'll just embrace a song
where love is always right
given freely,
even with bark and bite.
Is that wrong?
Goodnight.

EVEN IF THE MOUNTAINS WERE TO CRUMBLE AND THE HILLS DISAPPEAR, MY HEART OF STEADFAST, FAITHFUL LOVE WILL NEVER LEAVE YOU, AND MY COVENANT OF PEACE WITH YOU WILL NEVER BE SHAKEN," SAYS YAHWEH, WHOSE LOVE AND COMPASSION WILL NEVER GIVE UP ON YOU.

ISAIAH 54:10 TPT

MISSING

I'm missing.
Absent without your presence.
Thoughts leave me in search of you.
My right mind left.

Sleep is restless
dreams, senseless, useless
Even there, there is no you.
There is no me.
My subconscious rejects the idea of a simile.

I am speechless, only in that I speak less,
in fear, my words may betray me, call out your name
that my lips may yet deceive me, and crave yours again.
Memories are the enemy I refuse to entertain.

They haunt with your mystery and magic.
While reality sits silent,
waiting,
ever-present,
tragic.
I am absent
mindedly fighting a battle that can't be won.
White flag, full mast, I surrender, I lose.
Lost, confused, I am missing.
Because I am missing you.

EVEN IF I HAVE TO ROAM THROUGH EVERY STREET, NOTHING WILL KEEP ME FROM MY SEARCH. WHERE IS HE—MY SOUL'S TRUE LOVE? HE IS NOWHERE TO BE FOUND.

SONG OF SONGS 3:2 TPT

LOVE STILL LIVES

The degree of one's deliberate sacrificial selflessness or the lack thereof is a measure of the depth of that person's love. Time is the only commodity that cannot be collected or recovered. Great friends are big spenders with their time. In the Fall of 2016, I broke the bank. I spent nearly every free moment with Eli, one of my oldest and most cherished friends. In close circles, the proper name was "Eli and Isha." Amongst friends and family, it was always "they," not "he" or "she." They were inseparable since High School. They were the couple everyone loved or would love to be.

In High School, Eli and I were like twins separated at birth. Not that we looked alike. We were band geeks and shared the goofy, mischievous sense of humor that bordered on silly and senseless—the smack in the back of your head when the teacher isn't looking kind of playfulness. Sometimes we couldn't tell if others were laughing with us or laughing at us. There was never a time that we cared.

Eli was a drummer who played as if he came out of the womb with drumsticks in hand. I played the trumpet like a dunce with amusia and little to no enthusiasm, my rebellion for a closed choral list, and teen angst. In appearance, we were opposites. Eli was already six feet tall, with a football player build, flawless bronze skin. His smile was almost as bright as mine—much more handsome than any high school dork is expected to be. I was 5'6" with a bit of an hourglass shape taking form, fair-skinned such that some of the Black kids called me "Casper," a face peppered with pimples, and green eyes most insisted were contact lenses. He was naturally well-mannered, with the biggest heart and the 6th sense ability to discern people and their motives. He had no tolerance nor patience for superficiality. It was this that brought us together as friends.

In the first few weeks of sophomore year, I wasn't the first person one chooses for a friend. I had a bitter chip on my shoulder, with more anguish than any 14-year-old should carry, and an anvil of arrogance where a hope-filled heart should have been. Eli saw through it all. On a Tuesday in October, while leaving band class, he stopped directly in front of me, looked me square in the eyes, and paused. I was ready to spit a vicious response expecting him to ask if my eyes were contacts. But, instead, he grabbed my trumpet case, convinced me to skip lunch in the cafeteria, sneak out the school's back door, and get pizza. I can't remember what we talked about, but we laughed so much, drinks came out of our noses. From that day on, he was one of the few people that could lead me back to my best self when I felt miserable. I became the sister he never had. He became the brother I never knew I needed.

I always took credit for the creation of "Eli and Isha." When Eli and I were together, our body language made it evident that we were more like siblings than anything else. So, it made sense for any girl to think him available. Isha was beautiful, with a sense of innocence and coy simultaneously. I noticed her gazing at him while walking the halls a number of times. Each time I directed his attention to her, she became a shrinking violet. I found out that she was a bit of a church mouse, bookworm, and in all advanced classes. She seemed to be a good match for him.

Over time there was a change in his gait and posture whenever he saw her. The silent dance of the eyes they did was amusing. I grew impatient, waiting for someone to make the first move. Finally, winter break grew near, and I could not handle the suspense and so refused to wait to connect them. So, I walked to her in a bold, less than graceful manner and told her to come with us for ice cream after school. She sheepishly agreed to go if I planned to be there. After the last class, I pretended to have horrible cramps and need to go home. The rest was history.

Eli was the kind of guy that every mother and grandmother adored. Every father and grandfather respected and had pride in. We all loved Isha. She was a natural fit in all of our lives. Intelligent, gentle, kind, ambitious, and generous. She grew more beautiful as the years passed. Everyone from Eli's mother up to the greatgrands gave her the thumbs up.

Over the years, we stayed connected through college, grad school, careers, and life of "adulting." We always celebrated each other's wins and showed up for the "wonts." However, as time passed, schedules got tighter, often misaligned. We meant to get together, schedule double dates. We toyed with the idea of us all taking a group vacation for the better part of a year but never found the time. In one day, everything changed. Eli called, sounding like someone I have never known. Through the cries, I could not understand the details of what happened, but I heard the pain in his voice. A sound all too familiar. I canceled my plans and headed out the door.

When I arrived at the house, I was met by a sobbing huddled mass. The energy felt as if every heart that ever broke was rotting somewhere nearby. It was a sad sight. For the next several hours, I was given the "she said," "he said," the "when I knew I was in love," the fights, the make-ups, the proposal, the breakup, and now, the end. I watched, listened, and teared up as he laughed, cried, got angry, cursed, threw things, broke them, wept, smiled, fell silent, and finally fell asleep. I was exhausted. I went to the bedroom to grab a blanket for him. I noticed the empty spaces on the dresser, bare racks on one side of their walk-in closet, and an empty drawer slightly ajar—then I felt hollow as well.

Back in the den, I covered his massive frame as best as I could. I settled on the other couch and reflected on the years. I wished I'd been a better friend and felt guilty that I hadn't made more effort to stay connected. I hate seeing people in the kind of pain that a pill can't fix. I sank deeper into the pillows on the couch and relaxed, letting my thoughts and eyes drift around the room. There were countless mementos and photos of a gorgeous couple deeply in love, art from exotic vacations, and the snoring remnant of my crushed, tough-guy-turned-tortoise friend. I thought of how heavy his heart is right now. His life changed in one day.

The next few days, weeks, and months will be heartbreaking as he restructures his life without her. Morning showers without her jumping in, Sunday brunch without her stealing strawberries from his pancakes, and events without her on his arm will be torturous. I grabbed a trash bag and began collecting what looked like Kleenex fallout. Then, a thought occurred to me. This connection was a love so rich that it became ingrained in the very essence of his existence, so deep that it could bring someone so big and strong to his knees, what he thought was the end of him. Some people would kill to know the feeling, such an intense connection with another. The loss must feel like death. But to have his capacity; an open heart, receptive, vulnerable, selflessly loving, and able to fully committed to another person is wealth—worth more than many people can offer or deservedly receive.

In the days that followed, there was more replaying of events as he recalled, arrogant yelling peppered with "she must have lost her mind." and 1 am phone calls of drunken sadness. It was months before Eli was no longer the undercover "sick puppy" in our circle of friends and nurtured back to health. While my heart aches for him, I know well there can be bliss on the other side of madness. Even if tomorrow is not the morning that joy is restored. He loved, deeply, vulnerably, with passionate commitment. That is what his heart is capable of, what he can give, and what he can receive. That is who he is. Having that strength and intensity of love will forever be yours. When love is who you are, love you will always have, even if memories of moments seem bigger than your heart will ever be.

"I MISS YOUR VOICE BECAUSE IT IS A SYMPHONY; YOUR SCENT BECAUSE IT IS A TREASURE; YOUR SMILE BECAUSE IT IS A JEWEL; YOUR HUG BECAUSE IT IS A MASTERPIECE, AND YOUR KISS BECAUSE IT IS A MIRACLE."

— *MATSHONA DHLIWAYO*

SMOKE

Sitting ever so still
breath baited,
oblivious to all but the dream.
Anticipation weighted

On edge,anxious,
phone in hand, he, fully charged,
waiting, her text, praying, her call,
longing for the deep hypnosis
provoked by the melody that is her voice.

Like the full moons tide, his hope swells
floods him with memories of her energy
breeching the levy of futile resistance
daring the destiny of the damned
washing away yesterday
leaving him only and all that he is
drenched, massive, swollen, solemn,
strengthened by this infirmity.
Her

He breathes, chest heaves.
inhales as if his first breath
and there she is, her scent
she is with him.

Ever present,
her essence lingers,
leaving him never more with
never more without
her.

Irritated,
she incessantly is,

in and around him,
all-encompassing.
Fully consumed, choked
with closed eyes, she is everywhere.

Open, his deep dark eyes call,
curse her absence, craving her presence,
longing for the lightning of her laughter,
the warmth of her smile,
the fire that singes his flesh
when she grazes his skin while fluttering by.

Her gentle touch, hands like an angel fluttered kiss
permeate his skin, enter into all of him,
taking hold of his soul.
He let go,
complete surrender,
weak from the angst of a lifetime without.
Her.

He lies,
his heart down, in tribute.
Joyful sacrifice,
a weight no more,
relieved, his hollow heart
a massive beast of burden
longing for anything,
everything that is of Her.

Distanced, she watches,
waiting, knowing, needing, aching.
Certain love nor loss will ever burn so deep
or reach his intensity
love lost, found waiting.
Goodbye, the last greet.
One meet would taint her exit
an ending crafted beautifully.

She leaves, no relief,
no rest, though weary.

Still
faithfully, she prays
a melody of pain and praise.

Faithfully, he stays,
waiting, ever so still,
breath baited,
oblivious to all but the dream.
A last glimpse of her
Unseen.

A pitiful grasp of hope
slowly dissipates,
like smoke.

EVEN IF YOU LIVE A LONG TIME, DON'T TAKE A SINGLE DAY FOR GRANTED. TAKE DELIGHT IN EACH LIGHT-FILLED HOUR, REMEMBERING THAT THERE WILL ALSO BE MANY DARK DAYS AND THAT MOST OF WHAT COMES YOUR WAY IS SMOKE.

ECCLESIASTES 11:7-8 MSG

GRACEFUL EXIT

Pain lurks
behind the smile
—acidic
—corrosive
A noxious odor no one detects
It stifles each attempted breath
fills lungs
—crushes your chest
suffocates you into submission
You gasp
choke
fight to hold on
Wondering
when it ends
The suffering
how long

They say pain is the feeling of weakness leaving the body.

There must be a more graceful exit.

EVEN IF DARKNESS OVERTAKES THEM, SUNRISE-BRILLIANCE WILL COME BURSTING THROUGH BECAUSE THEY ARE GRACIOUS TO OTHERS, SO TENDER AND TRUE.

PSALM 112:4 TPT

MEMORIES

Memories lost
like moments so divine,
waking you from a dream.
Suddenly.
Once the memories were all mine.

Eyes open to darkness
feeling around for what should be there
could be there closer—right here.

Where it's supposed to be,
where last they left me
memories.
so sweet

I still hear the tune of the taste,
still on a sugar high,
swaying in the breeze of memories.
unspoken good-byes
Dreams relieve temporarily
a soft place to fall.
Morning violates
sunlight dissipates
images of it all.

What's a dream without the memories?
What's memory without recall?
The sum of all that's left behind
nothing—nothing at all.

I HAVE SEEN THAT ALL THINGS HAVE AN END, EVEN IF THEY ARE PERFECT, BUT YOUR WORD IS WITHOUT END.

PSALM 119:96 NLV

WITH YOU

I died with you.
Left with you on my mind,
your name on my lips,
the taste of your kiss still sweet on my lips.
With the force of your chest
still pressed against my breast
I closed my eyes and died.

Nose filled with your scent
lips still on your neck
I took my last breath.

Eyes bronzed by rays of your smile.
Heart warmed by incessant heat,
skin pickled with goosebumps
—courtesy of your cool
smoothly, I slipped away
—gently sleep.

Radiating your glow,
cradled in unyielding arms.
My physical form dissipates,
Passing into a place of no return.
Forever. By you, charmed.

My tombstone will be you—the rock
ever-present obelisk.
the mark of a former me
confirmation of my ever after

sleep will be deep
dreams bittersweet
with fading memories

of an angel, winged in peace
She, who used to be
part of only you and me
will never again be seen

What's left—
Flesh.
A stranger in the mirror
I'm supposed to live in this
I guess

You will forever be my resting place
A place where there is no longer rest.

I died with you.
I left with you on my mind,
your name on my lips,
remembering your face pressed
against this face that's left.

Your essence, our "We."
will forever be.
I died with you; there is no next.
Just an empty frame,
a suit of flesh.
Here behind
where you left.

THEIR MEMORIES

If the sun won't rise
and the moon turns to fire
the sky begins to bleed
water turns live wire

My eyes will ever be on you
My heart forever needs you
I pray the Lord's comfort be released
My mind will never cease
searching for you.

Acceptance? No.
They still force me to breathe
frozen in disbelief
anything but you
can be taken away from me.

Even fools keep memories.
Each thought demands
you being redeemed.
Your rightful place—
my heart, my hands.
the "You and Me."
It's not that hard to see.

It's said, at some point, you
must let go—I say no

I'm held, hostage
in every dream
waking shaken up
because it's just me

Their understanding,
no concern of mine.
They all think I've lost my mind.

“And that's OK”
A therapist would say.
It's a small price to pay.

What's the use of a mind
consumed by yesterday.
The silent soul inside me,
is still determined to pray
He’ll make a way.

But now I ask—
What exactly am I supposed to do?
Live like it's OK
there is no more you?

Can you see them?
Going on—
like something in me has gone wrong
life continues, yes,
but without you
—time lasts far too long
I know—I'm not that strong
What's wrong is that you're forever gone.
Their memories don’t last long.

Now I'm standing, long forlorn
in a world where I no longer belong.
If you must, be heaven bound
My hearts translation; gone
save me a seat beside you
to join heavens song.

EVEN IF I AM FAR AWAY FROM YOU IN BODY, I AM WITH YOU IN SPIRIT.

COLOSSIANS 2:5 NLV

ANOTHER NEVER

Nine years since you said goodbye,
to the pain and struggle.
I understand why.

Why the other side seemed brighter
To walk with a load a little lighter
You tapped out of this round
But you're still a damn good fighter.

Now it seems as though I walk alone
With a heartbroken and without a home.
I know your heart is finally free
from anguish most can't conceive.

So it was today when you said goodbye
to a plague of darkness toward a brighter light.
Those who know your story
stand with you, though we cry
we'll hold things down here
until we see you on the other side.

Many times I want to reach out to you
or call you just because.
In dreams, you come and comfort me
though I know it's sleep's mirage.

We'll bask in your glowing memory
while you dance with the angels of God.
There will never be another sister like you.
There will never be another Tajh.

EVEN IF THESE BODIES WE LIVE IN ARE FOLDED UP AT DEATH LIKE TENTS, WE WILL STILL HAVE A GOD-BUILT HOME THAT NO HUMAN HANDS HAVE BUILT, WHICH WILL LAST FOREVER IN THE HEAVENLY REALM.

2 CORINTHIANS 5:1 TPT

GET UP

Even if you are in the 12th round
buckled bent back over the ropes
ears ringing
crowds screaming
eyes are bleeding
ready for it all to end
body broken, all skills—nil
bloody
covered in burning cuts that sting from within
do not lay down.
Do not give up.
The fight is not over until you win.

EVEN IF THEY FIGHT AGAINST YOU, THEY WILL NOT GET POWER OVER YOU. FOR I AM WITH YOU TO SAVE YOU AND BRING YOU OUT OF TROUBLE," SAYS THE LORD.

JEREMIAH 15:20 NLV

PATIENCE

I called friends.
They did not come.
I waited.
Patience produced no one.

The coming storm is here.
There is not much that scares.
It's easier to hold back fear
when those who have your back are near.

Patience produced no one.
Were they sleeping?
Did they walk away?
Was I calling the wrong people
or in the wrong way?

Storms are never weathered
crying for brighter days and sun.
Wars are never won
wishing for ammo and guns.
Patience produced no one.

Patience proved useless
friendships fruitless.
Grace, though torched by fire
it still produces pardons.
Was it like that in the garden?

EVEN IF THEY SIN AGAINST YOU SEVEN TIMES IN A DAY AND SEVEN TIMES COME BACK TO YOU SAYING 'I REPENT,' YOU MUST FORGIVE THEM.

LUKE 7:4 NIV

ORDINARY

They say I've changed
suddenly, acting strange
they say.
Truth is
I have always been this way.
Ever-changing, evolving.
They stay the same.

The real strange is, as times change
old ways and stagnant minds remain.
Funny that it makes me the strange one.
I'll project no blame.

There are words I no longer say
places I'd never stay
games I no longer play.
Newness operates that way
hard for a purview focused down and away

It's OK. They drift, I have a new direction.
Intimacy may change
Affection remains with
portended sustained connections
conjecture and kind expression feigned.

Goodbyes aren't difficult
when flooded with a new Hi, heartfelt.
A new love helps forget old lies
and boredom of ordinary
after extraordinary enters life.

It cuts the ties
to useless, previously unrecognized
colossal wastes of time.

Extraordinary overshadows mediocrity.
If that's the change, they call strange
not better than, much better off
I choose an extraordinary life.
The only constant is change.

EVEN IF THEY TALK AGAINST YOU AS WRONG-DOERS, IN THE END THEY WILL GIVE THANKS TO GOD FOR YOUR GOOD WORKS WHEN CHRIST COMES AGAIN.

1 PETER 2:12 NLV

SMILE

I woke up
So the good Lord smiled on me
Before I opened my eyes
I smiled back gratefully.

MY PEOPLE WILL LIVE IN SAFETY, QUIETLY AT HOME. THEY WILL BE AT REST. EVEN IF THE FOREST SHOULD BE DESTROYED AND THE CITY TORN DOWN, THE LORD WILL GREATLY BLESS HIS PEOPLE.

ISAIAH 32:18-20 NLT

ONE DAY

One day
Maybe someday
If all goes right and one way
Not left, nor left behind.
No reverse toward yesterday

Tomorrow—an ephemeral prospect
a nebulous concept.
Guarantee is deceit.

But a promise
worth reflection.
An indemnified prospection
a substantiated conjecture
a guarantor, given assurances
is that protection?

Unseen hope on papered promises
seen by a known witness?
Tomorrow. A gift.
Is that what this is?
Is this the path to where wisdom is?

Show the way.
Can I write it down?
Is it best to know by heart?
Is this the place, or the part
when the happy endings start?

With clocks designed without man's hands
in hearts purposed with new parts
is now when morning starts

when days have no end
when wisdom rules hearts?

Yesterday – gone and left.
An undelayed fade.
Lost—Not without recourse
Debt demanding it be paid.

But grace—An execution stayed.
An irrevocable trust—faith.
Vanishing prints of yesterday
Judgment and justice—displaced

From days long forlorn,
beyond expiration
even now is gone

A new footprint paves
A way, a patient wait
New light and new sight can see
Alas, tomorrow is a place.

EVEN IF YOU ARE EXILED TO THE ENDS OF THE EARTH, I WILL BRING YOU BACK TO THE PLACE I HAVE CHOSEN FOR MY NAME TO BE HONORED.

NEHEMIAH 1:9 NLT

FOREVER FRIENDS

I didn't believe him.
Not at first.
What's hard
is it seemed like just seconds passed
things started getting worse.
I was looking for the truth.
Why did it hurt?
Enough to make you curse.
I didn't.

I didn't want to create an environment
where if He came back
so we can try again
for me to trust
that there's an "I" in Him.
Not lies
just love between friends.
I hope that wasn't the end.

I thought and said all I knew
thought myself wise
I was rude.

If not my words, my actions asked
"Why should I trust you?"
"There will be no regrets if you do."
His reply, I wanted to hold on to.
If not all of me, then who?
He said, "Without me, there is no You."

I am glad He came back again.
Knocked gently,
and I let him in.

I said sorry for all the things I said.
“Your sorry is what makes
all of those things dead.”

He grabbed my hand
kissed my forehead.
“The other way is the dead end.”
He said.
“Now we're forever friends.
With me, there is no end.”

EVEN IF WE FEEL GUILTY, GOD IS GREATER THAN OUR FEELINGS, AND HE KNOWS EVERYTHING.

1 JOHN 3:20 NLT

HE'S HERE

When I wake up
He's right there.
Jesus.
Did you know that?
Right here.

Beside me. Behind me.
Above me. Before me.
In case I don't notice,
he sets out new gifts
just for me.
Grace and mercy,
things I can't miss.

He's like that.
New ones every day.
When I can't get up,
He covers me up
—That's his way.

When I can't get out
He carries me
most often to my knees
before I can reach the coffee.

He knows I can hear him better down there.
Here, on my knees.
we hear each other clearly here.

When I wake up since He's right here,
I meet him, often on my knees.
I bring my fear, details of every nightmare.
He says he knows; He was there.

"I woke you up, so you could see
I Am right here, gathering your tears."
It doesn't always look that way to me.
"I am still here, attentive to every prayer."

He says, "When you wake up, fear not
I Am right here. There is no other possibility.
Trust me. Not what your eyes can see.
They are not, nor is anything stronger than me."

'Wherever you go, I Am there.
I Love You. More than anyone can dare to.
More than anyone can care too.
Always. Forever. I Am right here.
All of me, for all of you."

"Beside you. Behind you.
Above you. Before you.
You are my child.
This, I will forever do
never leave you nor forsake you
All of me, for all of you."

THE LORD HIMSELF GOES BEFORE YOU AND WILL BE WITH YOU; HE WILL NEVER LEAVE YOU NOR FORSAKE YOU. DO NOT BE AFRAID; DO NOT BE DISCOURAGED. BE STRONG AND COURAGEOUS. DO NOT BE AFRAID OR TERRIFIED BECAUSE OF THEM, FOR THE LORD YOUR GOD GOES WITH YOU; HE WILL NEVER LEAVE YOU NOR FORSAKE YOU.

DEUTERONOMY 31:8, DEUTERONOMY 31:6 NIV

ALL

You figured me out for me.
I didn't have a clue.
Another one of those things you do
You being you.

I think I'm better that way,
even if just better off.
There are lines no one should ever cross.
But you hide me behind the cross,
cover me, and dust me off.
You being you,
another thing that you do
that leaves me better off.

I'm never lost.
You find me when I can't find myself.
When I've lost my right mind, I'm never left.
I don't look back; you're always behind,
me, at any cost.

Some might say this is love.
Others may call it sacrifice. I say it's life.
A real life, one worth living, is filled with love.
Real love, love worth living for, is filled with sacrifice.

You could count the days and read every page
in the book that is my life.
Exhibit A, untainted evidence
of your love, life, and sacrifice.

Reasonably, unreasonable
unquestionably,

absent of doubt
hands red, your guilt made me innocent,
set right.
You being you.

I'm better off, never lost.
Your light finds my feet, and I find myself home,
but then in places, I don't belong.
I go a way; maybe I shouldn't have gone.
You set me upright when I'm not right
and cover my wrongs.

How long is “I'll never leave you”?
Does “lo, I'm with you always” have an end date?
A “No.” I always love to hear you say
So, I say yes, every day.

I say yes when my feet feel they might stray.
My soul says yes,
your light still Finds my feet.
Where can I go when my heart's home is you,
there can be no other way.

Your heart is my home, no matter where I roam.
Your light still finds my feet.
I am yours alone
and your light is all I need.
In you, Jesus, I am home.

EVEN IF YOU HAVE BEEN BANISHED TO THE MOST DISTANT LAND UNDER THE HEAVENS, FROM THERE THE LORD YOUR GOD WILL GATHER YOU AND BRING YOU BACK.

DEUTERONOMY 30:5 NIV

TURN THE PAGE

Even if you lost everything—I have.
Left with struggle, strain, and strife
there is another side of the situation.
Expect there is still light and life.

Even if it seems our world is left in ash
do you think we are at the end?
It's part of the path; we can't see the win
in the wait
past the place where the path bends.

Even if it feels like your back
is pressed against a wall
know that rock and hard place rules nothing
—surely not our all.

You may squint and close your eyes.
But remember you have sight.
Even if day after day
seems like nothingness,
and cold, dark, anxious nights.

There is one ready to be a guide
despite lying eyes saying there is no light.
It seems we're hanging, barely by a thread
dangled over terrifying heights.
Still, I trust the higher one
inconceivably making all things right.

Who will catch me when the fall starts?
Without signal nor service, it's God I call.
Expectant for the future,
join me in line, despite this free fall.

Many are the afflictions of the righteous,
The Lord delivers them from them all.

I am holding on.
You can grab my hand.
God made rocks, hard places, and me.
I call him—because I know I can.
To come and get me, His child.
He says that I am.

I know I cannot face this at all,
There is nowhere to turn but up to you
—I'll wait.
Send more strength
I'm all out of mine
I need to see your face.

Bring on the other side.
Shine downlight, the glow of your Glory
Lift the cloak of darkness in this place.
I know He won't ignore me.

This broken and contrite heart calls up.
We have not reached the end of the story.
Salvation lies on the other side of the wait.
From faith comes deliverance for you and for me.

FOR THE HOLY SPIRIT MAKES GOD'S FATHERHOOD REAL TO US AS HE WHISPERS INTO OUR INNERMOST BEING, "YOU ARE GOD'S BELOVED CHILD!" AND SINCE WE ARE HIS TRUE CHILDREN, WE QUALIFY TO SHARE ALL HIS TREASURES, FOR INDEED, WE ARE HEIRS OF GOD HIMSELF. AND SINCE WE ARE JOINED TO CHRIST, WE ALSO INHERIT ALL THAT HE IS AND ALL THAT HE HAS. WE WILL EXPERIENCE BEING CO-GLORIFIED WITH HIM PROVIDED THAT WE ACCEPT HIS SUFFERINGS AS OUR OWN.

ROMANS 8:16-18

FAITH

My war stance.
It is my amour, my weapon, my shield.
I give the one true God honor.
To no other name do I yield.

For thine is the Glory
and honor above all.
My rock and salvation, your name, my fortress
Jesus, the strong towering wall.

Jesus – my War Cry.
Your name, none higher.
Standing firm before all enemies
I watch you rain down fire.

Your faithful unfazed,
unchanged ancient of days.
My voice, cry, plead, and prayer
you clearly hear every time I call.
In feast, famine, flood, plague, or war
there is no one and nothing greater,
none other than my Lord.

Jesus, your love remains.
My Jesus, how you never change.
"Jesus," My redeemers' name.
In faith, I stand victorious, all enemies amazed.

The pain you bared upon the cross.
You shed your blood and reclaimed your lost.
My God, you paid the highest cost.
My faith response: I surrender all.

Pain, I surrender, Lord.
Fear, I submit, take it Lord.
Doubt, I surrender Lord.
The name of Jesus, stronger than it all.

Sickness, I surrender, Lord.
Broken hearts are yours to reform.
Your love, my rescue in any storm.
When I wake, I put a faith shield on?

A mighty fortress when the battle is too long.
There is no greater power, no force more strong.
Keeping no account of all my wrongs.
So secure, the everlasting arms I lean on.

Faith—forever my war stance
my armor, my weapon, my shield
for thine is the glory, honor, dominion, and power,
to whom or what would my faith ever yield?

PRAISE V. PAIN

Prayer is more powerful than problems.
Praise speaks louder than pain.
Worship wages war on worry.
Fear is no match for faith.

God's promises are my foundation of peace.
No sickness will steal my song.
God tares down tumors and cancels cancer.
So devil, be gone.

A doctor's report will be heard.
But God, with all power, has the final word.
I will not bow or be bound by a deadly thing.
I kneel before the one true King.

So prayer will be my posture.
I will stand in a position of faith.
And I will worship in my darkest day.
I'm about that life of praise.

FAITH MEANS BEING SURE OF THE THINGS WE HOPE FOR. AND FAITH MEANS KNOWING THAT SOMETHING IS REAL EVEN IF WE DO NOT SEE IT.

HEBREWS 11:1 ICB

THE LORD IS

The Lord is the God of all creation
beyond earth and sea and sky.
He is the answer to
"I wonder how what, or why."

The Lord is greater than any and everything.
Our finite minds can't comprehend,
the infinite
but His Spirit speaks
—Without end.
The song my heart sings on repeat.

The Lord is not just a story
in the big old book on Grandma's table.
The Lord is not a plastic baby on a tattered lawn or mall manger
at Christmas time.
He is the only one that is able
to do anything and everything
—except fail or lie.

He's not the warm fuzzy feeling
when you're singing those non-Christ "Christmas" songs.
He is the Master of the ages.
He'll be back before long.
—You might want to get busy – doing something
worthwhile with the time – time He gave you.
Disagree?
What if you're wrong?

He's not the X in X-Mas.
Frankly, that concept is a mess.
Or the joyous feeling near a gorgeous tree
almost reaching the ceiling
Uprooted from nature

pronounced dead by New Years
covered in lights, tinsel,
and what – in two days – will just be trash.
Remembered, maybe in a picture.
Forever reduced to ash.

More dust in the wind.

He is. The I AM, that was, and is, and is to come.
The virgin-born, God with us, died, willingly
life sacrifice, and He is risen,
Why? Love.

To reclaim something,
there has to be a trade
you have to give; it will be a sacrifice.
For us, it is his life—He gave
—every drop of His blood.

Oh, the Blood of Jesus.

He is the only begotten Son of God.
Some of the things I say and do might be odd.
Would you expect a child of God
—to be ordinary?
Being ordinary—
the reclaimed daughter of the Living King
—ordinary is not part of the job.

My job, perhaps, is to help you see.
Let's take the blinders off.
Feel free to look right past me.
Can you conceive
the maker of heaven and earth
who set the sun's schedule and the moon's flow
create from dust and returns to dust, all things?
Where did you think they go?

Everything ends up hevel in hovels.
What's in your outer place storage space?
Be sure to outline the details,
the devil is hiding there.
But trust and believe he is not the one you should fear.
Since I see that you have an ear,
let me clarify for you, dear.

It's essential that you see
Him, not me.
And please believe
that your life, as you know it,
it has no warranty.

So when you reach the end of your road,
weighted with burdens, regrets by the load
and you close your weary eyes
that last time
what will you see?

This part is important.
It's going to be on the test.
I have some notes you can read.
They are in the Bible.
I strongly advise you to give it your best.

He did.

EVEN IF IT WAS WRITTEN IN SCRIPTURE LONG AGO, YOU CAN BE SURE IT'S WRITTEN FOR US. GOD WANTS THE COMBINATION OF HIS STEADY, CONSTANT CALLING AND WARM, PERSONAL COUNSEL IN SCRIPTURE TO COME TO CHARACTERIZE US, KEEPING US ALERT FOR WHATEVER HE WILL DO NEXT. MAY OUR DEPENDABLY STEADY AND WARMLY PERSONAL GOD DEVELOP MATURITY IN YOU SO THAT YOU GET ALONG WITH EACH OTHER AS WELL AS JESUS GETS ALONG WITH US ALL. THEN WE'LL BE A CHOIR—NOT OUR VOICES ONLY, BUT OUR VERY LIVES SINGING IN HARMONY IN A STUNNING ANTHEM TO THE GOD AND FATHER OF OUR MASTER JESUS!

ROMANS 15:4-6 MSG

FREEDOM

Your freedom was bled for.
Crown of thorns on his head for
Your freedom, eternal death
defeated.
What Jesus rose from the dead for.

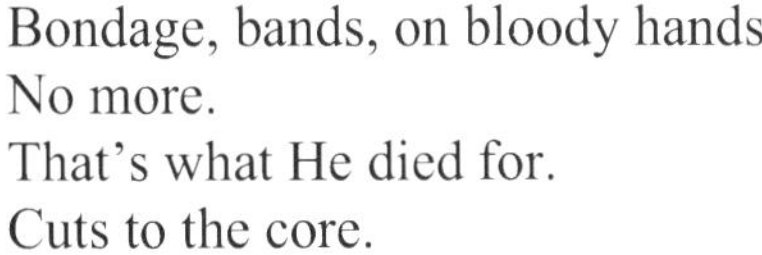

Bondage, bands, on bloody hands
No more.
That's what He died for.
Cuts to the core.

The challenge is
there's an imbalance in
where we get our knowledge from
parents, school, books, college, some.

Social media
For some, that's the only one.
Endless choices of news sources
Where is truth, knowledge, understanding, or wisdom?

We expect crowns.
Yes, we're royal
Trample on blessings all around.
We're not loyal.

We were hand-picked
Not for picnics but a palace
But mistake fallacy for reality
And want wealth without challenge.

Want pleasure without pain
Accolades for the mundane

Transformation but refuse to change
Elevation to standings you can't sustain.

Sit on fake thrones, in fake frames,
in cameras, on phones.
Place blame when things are rearranged
when your style of life is not the same.

You only cry for God,
when the world you knew seems odd
when helpless
sick, lost, or alone.
In silence, you suffer violence, defeated
battling with no army of your own
destined to be damned
when there's no King in your home.

EVEN IF A KING HAD THE BEST-EQUIPPED ARMY, IT WOULD NEVER BE ENOUGH TO SAVE HIM. EVEN IF THE BEST WARRIOR WENT TO BATTLE, HE COULD NOT BE SAVED SIMPLY BY HIS STRENGTH ALONE.

PSALM 33:16 TPT

WALK WITH HIM

I am draped in the blood of Jesus.
Wrapped and swaddled in
His Love, Grace, and Mercy
Devils may try to curse me,
they can't touch me nor hurt me.
My Father made me worthy.

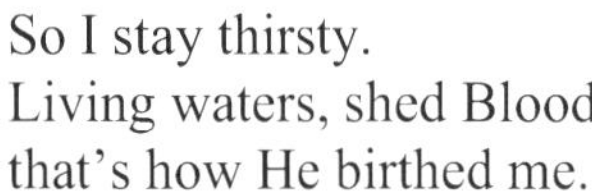

So I stay thirsty.
Living waters, shed Blood
that's how He birthed me.

His life, how else can I live.
My life, what else can I give?
Mind, body, spirit, and soul,
take it all, excavate this vessel.
Only you make me whole.

My past, unknown knowns,
burnt ash.
A new heart and new home
my destination, a golden path.

But right here, here is the hustle.
For you, I'll run on broken glass.
My Love for you
and the weight of this world clash.
But you, always, forever hold me fast.

Despite every fall,
when I ran, hid, fled,
my soul rotting inside me, dead.
If not for your life, for every word you said,
mind lost, dead outside and in
because I didn't make you head.

There were demons demands
bondage from bloody hands
shame, hate, abandoned faith.
How could I stand?
You grabbed my hand.

Before I could even walk
before Buchanan's and Bobbitt's had thoughts
before the devil's snare had me caught
inside the womb is where you taught.

Planted seeds in me—only you can grow.
Told me mysteries—only you could know.
Made me curious—for what only you can show.
And now, eyes see, ears hear,
to whom would I go?

I am all yours—
and you, are you, all by yourself.
When I was called — a lost cause
You – were all of my help.

I found the love letters you wrote
— to me.
Tears welled up inside me
— a monsoon of hope.
God is Dope.

There is no rope
for me to be at the end of.
I'm holding onto He who won't drop me
not an imitation or failed copies.
What can stop me?
My God's got me.

Tornados ripping up old trash
picking up the loose

the useless unnecessaries
That stuff we kept in stash.

You are faithful to the fallen
even when we keep falling off
My God — Jesus
The highest cost

Not some purse, whip, watch or trip
But the cross you carried, and endured the whip
for me, for us, for you, for we
For we are not our own anymore.
Living waters, your shed blood,
can I just have a sip?

I can't sit, stand, or kneel.
My only posture is face down on the ground.
That's still not reverent enough.
My words can't honor, your glory
But I beg for just a touch.

Just a touch – of the hem
of the garment – of my best friend
I can't wait until the end; I need you now.

This moment, right here
because you catch tears.
You make my smile fire.
Give me rest when I'm tired.

I'm so tired —
can I lean on your arms
Others – I've tried it.
They smile, only mean me harm.
I don't buy it.

You—are where I live
My life—that's what I give.

There is nothing that is mine
—— It's all his.

Earth, moon, wind, waves, and stars
you, me ——
all made in his image.
—Do you know who you are?

He said, here's life.
You're no longer dead.
You are set right —
Because that's what I said.

Were you there before He rose
Before being enthroned in heaven
Crown of thorns resting on his head?
My sin—was ——
But now—my sin is dead.

Despite all sorrow —
My sin is still dead tomorrow.
Despite the wrong that I intended to do
He hears my cries when I holler.

When I moan—when I scream
when my only prayer is tears that stream
when I thought heaven was just a dream
when I was blind to him
and to others, I was just mean
He still saw me and said,
—— She's with me.

Determined to reclaim me
from a world that bruised and maimed me.
Never once thought I was too damaged
too guilty, too dirty. He thought me worthy.

You can't see wind – it uproots trees

knocks down buildings and tears off chimneys.

You can't see it or touch it,
or peel it, or pluck it.
You can't put wind, or Him
— in an empty bucket.
My zeal, Him in me
You can't measure how much.
It is.

He never runs out —
When we run away – He's on the other side.
Don't you dare for a minute doubt
to lavish and love us,
that's the business that he's in.
God is Love, baby.
That's what He's all about.

I don't need His resume.
He wrote the book.
No matter what I do, or where I go, or what I say
If I turn up and say and mean, I am sorry
Past sin, last year or yesterday, or this morning,
He won't even look —
It's right here in the book.

In here,
the Love Letter He wrote us.
Came to fix us, where people broke us.
Change my mind when I start to feel hopeless
The only price —
is that I stay focused.

On Him —
He who forgives all sin
Roll with Him —
he never fails, so all I do is win.

When I first started walking with Him
I tripped, stumbled, and fell, to just begin.
Drank, smoked, went to all kinds of places I shouldn't have been.
But when I looked up in repentance
He looked down and said —
You're still in.

Walk with him —
He's the only way, the only truth, the only light,
I was born wrong,
and wrong was sometimes how I lived my life.
And I am still wrapped and swaddled in Him
—my re-birth right.
Cause I'm with Him.
Are you ready to begin?

Just say, "Yes, Lord. I see you now.
Jesus, I hear your call.
My sin, my shame, my hurt, the blame,
Lord, please, erase it all."

"Lord, my door is open, please
— open yours."
"Put my name on your list
Lord, can I get in?' —

Tell the Lord—"I am ready,
I am ready to begin."
Walk with Him.

If you said those words —
— Outside or in
Confession – hand raise "Lord, I sin.
That's the state I used to live in."
now you belong
— to Him

So expect to see and hear Him,
draw near —— to Him
He Loves you; no fear in Him
Welcome to the family.
You're in.

Now —— He walks with you.
Walk with Him.

THEY WERE TALKING WITH EACH OTHER ABOUT EVERYTHING THAT HAD HAPPENED. AS THEY TALKED AND DISCUSSED THESE THINGS WITH EACH OTHER, JESUS HIMSELF CAME UP AND WALKED ALONG WITH THEM.

LUKE 24:14-15 NIV

BE THE SONG

Years after she passed, I had a vibrant dream of my sister Tajh. I have always been a vivid dreamer. They are colorful, memorable, and multi-sensory. But this dream was unique.

We were about five and seven years old, dancing and jumping around in what seemed like a glowing white bouncy house—a bubble of our own. Without music, we danced and laughed like the only thing that mattered was the fun of that moment. We jumped around as silly as two unsupervised children on a sugar high.

She sat down smiling. I kept dancing while she continued grinning and giggling as if my happy dance was the most entertaining thing in the world. I felt free, happy, without a care in the world. I was filled with joy as if sunshine was radiating from inside while light brighter than sunshine surrounded us. The dream seemed like a peek into a heavenly play space.

It has been more than 30 years since I laughed so hard, danced so freely, and felt like being her funny baby sister was the most important endeavor. God always knows what we need, when we need it, and how we need it. There is so much peaceful symbolism in the dream that I feel a warmth every time I think of it. Seemingly, a visit just when I need the reminder; keep dancing even if the music stops—be the song. Thank you, Tajh. Keep shining.

EVEN IF THE MUSIC STOPS
BE THE SONG.

FOR THE LOVE OF TAJH

SISTERS ON ASSIGNMENT

A sibling is often your first and longest best friend. Tajh was my first best friend, yet we could not have been more opposite. When we were older, our relationship could have been likened to oil and water at times. We are all born into a family that we did not choose. Sometimes, families, we would never choose. Fortunately, we have the family and friends assigned, friends we choose who become family. These relationships are closer and more cherished than any other they come to know.

Tajh was blessed to have had the family that she chose. They loved her tremendously. I use the term assigned sisters—those who are like angels who walk alongside us. Throughout our lives, carry us when we fall, celebrate with us in good times, cry when we cry, and fight for us against any enemy. Tajh had an assigned family. Some were closer to her than anyone, a group of friends who cherished and adored her. Yet, more than ten years later, they are all still devastated and heartbroken by her absence. I could not close this book without honoring her and her chosen family. Each year, they remember her with messages posted on her memorial page.

As she lives in their hearts forever, I have included shared memories and messages posted over the years to honor their love for her. As you read them, I pray that you know and never forget that people love you more than you imagine. There are people you have yet to meet who you will love, who will love you more than you can fathom. Remember, you are a gift from God – sent from heaven. God issued the mandate that you be present in the world and a present to the world. So, to you, my heaven-sent twin, I love you, God loves you. Now is an excellent time to celebrate. I vote for lattes and chocolate cake!

MEMORIES LIVE LIKE PEOPLE DO.

—*UNKNOWN*

FOREVER REMEMBERED

JOYCE: From the first time I met Tajh, she was attached to me. For some reason I couldn't let her go. She was a good girl. She was just like me, both of our birthdays are in February. So we wore our emotions on our sleeves. She was emotional, got her feelings hurt easily, just like me. She was always my best friend. She was always there. Anytime I needed her, she was there.

She always had a hustle, two and three jobs lined up at a time, ready to go always. Selling on eBay and at pop-up shops. She loved music. She was DJing, her DJ name was DJ MUSIQ, even sold her CDs. She always had a waitress job, different kinds of restaurants. She loved being a waitress.

We would always go out to the club. CCs was our favorite because they played mostly house music. We always had so much fun, just me and Tajh. We would dance our butts off, like they say, like nobody's watching. Just me and Tajh. We would dance sweating; I mean SWEATING and dancing. We'd stay out, and have so much fun.

One time, she was having a party at her house. Oh my God, we had the best time. We went to her house, everybody was singing, every time a song came up we were singing. Tajh had her song, she played it over and over again. We kept singing, I don't know how long. It was probably one of the best parties we ever went to.

Tajh had cats, loved her cats. When we heard what happened, some went to her house and saw she laid out so much water and cat food. I guess she knew what she was going to do beforehand. But she made sure her cats were going to be OK.

I'll never have another best friend like that. I have great friends; I have had a lot of good friends. I know she was my best friend when she lived. I'll probably never have another best friend like Tajh. Well, I hope I do. I know I won't.

I love you Tajh. —Joyce August 2021

Tajh was a true light in this world, so misunderstood but still pressed forward... I saw a lot of me in her and always wanted to connect with her to try to guide her. But Tajh was strong willed and did things her way and how can you not have respect for that. A young woman coming into her own. I truly miss her and wish she could see my daughter now who Tajh lovingly called Mookie when she was a baby... Tajh I have so many stories about you, us, life, growth... Continue to sleep in power. The love I have for you I hope reaches you even where you are now in paradise. —Alexis August 4, 2021

Love you, Tajh! Miss you! –Joyce October 25, 2019

I miss her so much. I wish I could call her. God bless. – Cyndi October 25, 2019

Happy Birthday, my Sista Tajh. Another year and another tear. I think of you often, and I see your pic, and yet again, you are really missed. Rest in peace. And know you are always in my heart with everyone else. Till we meet again. Love you. – Cyndi February 1, 2018

To my dearest family member, Happy 40th Birthday!! It's still mind-blowing that your presence is not here. Spiritually you are. I love you, Tajh, and no one on this side of your family does not think of you, miss you, and most of all, LOVE You. Rest in peace. my Tajh. – Cyndi January 31, 2016

She was a kind soul – Valerie

Tajh was a one-of-a-kind human being that you were honored to have in your life. I cry and smile when I think of you. I love and miss you dearly. – Cyndi October 25, 2015

Only on this earth for a brief time, yet she touched the soul of everyone that she met. – Jessyca

Today is 8 years from when my dear friend and sister passed on. My dear Tajh, I love and miss you. I see your pic every morning with everyone else. I have no fear, for I have plenty of family I will get to see again when it's my time. Until then, rest in peace. Tajh, and know you are missed, blessed, and loved dearly. – Cyndi October 24, 2015

My best friend! Miss you so much! – Joyce October 19, 2015

Gone too soon, my friend! – Jessyca

I can't even look at her closeups without crying. That was my baby, and I still can't imagine the pain she was in at that point in her life. – Alexis October 24, 2015

A beautiful soul who is gone way too soon. Rest in peace. – Judy October 19, 2015

Still hard to believe you have gone, your heart was so big, and you were so loveable. I know there's a party going on up there! See you on the other side! Love you. – Jessica Lynn October 17, 2015

Tajh, you will never be forgotten. You will always be in our hearts, thoughts, and prayers. We miss your earthly presence! – Jessyca October 17, 2015

She is an angel watching over you! – Jessyca

FOR THE LOVE OF TAJH

FOREVER REMEMBERED

HELP IS AVAILABLE

If you or anyone you know is thinking of or has decided to commit suicide or has expressed the idea of suicide. Please connect with one of the resources listed immediately.

CALL

Emergency number 911 (US and Canada) 999 (UK)

National Suicide Prevention Lifeline 1-800-273-8255

The Lifeline provides 24/7, free and confidential support including Spanish-speakers and anyone who is deaf or hard of hearing.

Suicidepreventionlifeline.org

ONLINE CHAT https://suicidepreventionlifeline.org/chat/

TEXT

Crisis Text Line -- Text Hello to 741741 fields messages about suicidal thoughts, abuse, sexual assault, depression, anxiety, bullying, and more. You can text 741741 in the US or UK (686868 in Canada)

YOUTHLINE

Text teen2teen to 839863, or call 1-877-968-8491

BIBLICAL SCRIPTURE REFERENCE

Alphabetically by Poem

ALL

God has said, "Never will I leave you; never will I forsake you." Hebrews 13:5 NIV

Be strong and courageous. Do not be afraid or terrified because of them, for the Lord your God goes with you; he will never leave you nor forsake you." Deuteronomy 31:6 NIV

Even in darkness light dawns for the upright, for those who are gracious and compassionate and righteous. Psalm 112:4 NIV

And surely I am with you always, to the very end of the age." Matthew 28:20 NIV

DO OVER

For if, while we were God's enemies, we were reconciled to him through the death of his Son, how much more, having been reconciled, shall we be saved through his life! Not only is this so, but we also boast in God through our Lord Jesus Christ, through whom we have now received reconciliation. Romans 5:10-11 NIV

"Be silent before me, you islands! Let the nations renew their strength! Let them come forward and speak; let us meet together at the place of judgment. Isaiah 41:1 NIV

Your word is a lamp for my feet, a light on my path. Psalm 119:105 NIV

When Jesus spoke again to the people, he said, "I am the light of the world. Whoever follows me will never walk in darkness, but will have the light of life." John 8:12 NIV

The righteous cry out, and the Lord hears them; he delivers them from all their troubles. Psalm 34:17 NIV

But now, this is what the Lord says —he who created you, Jacob, he who formed you, Israel: "Do not fear, for I have redeemed you; I have summoned you by name; you are mine. Isaiah 43:1 NIV

EVEN IF

"Arise, shine, for your light has come, and the glory of the Lord rises upon you. See, darkness covers the earth and thick darkness is over the peoples, but the Lord rises upon you and his glory appears over you. Nations will come to your light, and kings to the brightness of your dawn. Isaiah 60:1-3 NIV

For I consider that the sufferings of this present time are not worth comparing with the glory that is to be revealed to us. Romans 8:18 ESV

FAITH

O Lord, You have great power, shining-greatness and strength. Yes, everything in heaven and on earth belongs to You. You are the King, O Lord. And You are honored as head over all. 1 Chronicles 29:11 NLV

If we tell Him our sins, He is faithful and we can depend on Him to forgive us of our sins. He will make our lives clean from all sin. 1 John 1:9 NLV

We are sure that if we ask anything that He wants us to have, He will hear us. 1 John 5:14 NLV

You are being kept by the power of God because you put your trust in Him and you will be saved from the punishment of sin at the end of the world. 1 Peter 1:5 NLV

The Lord watches over those who are right with Him. He hears their prayers. But the Lord is against those who sin." 1 Peter 3:12 NLV

God was in Christ. He was working through Christ to bring the whole world back to Himself. God no longer held men's sins against them. And He gave us the work of telling and showing men this. 2 Corinthians 5:19 NLV

For this reason You are great, O Lord God. There is none like You. And there is no God but You, by all that we have heard with our ears. 2 Samuel 7:22 NLV.

Keep a careful watch over yourselves and over the church. The Holy Spirit has made you its leaders. Feed and care for the church of God. He bought it with His own blood. Acts 20:28 NLV

Everything in heaven and on earth can come to God because of Christ's death on the cross. Christ's blood has made peace. Colossians 1:20 NLV

"As I kept looking, thrones were set up and the One Who has lived forever took His seat. His clothing was as white as snow and the hair of His head was like pure wool. His throne and its wheels were a burning fire. Daniel 7:9 NLV

'O Lord God, You have begun to show Your servant Your great power and Your strong hand. For what god is there in heaven or on earth who can do such works and powerful acts as You do? Deuteronomy 3:24 NLV

Because of the blood of Christ, we are bought and made free from the punishment of sin. And because of His blood, our sins are forgiven. His loving-favor to us is so rich. Ephesians 1:7 NLV

Put on the things God gives you to fight with. Then you will not fall into the traps of the devil. Ephesians 6:11 NLV

Most important of all, you need a covering of faith in front of you. This is to put out the fire-arrows of the devil. Ephesians 6:16 NLV

Christ bought us with His blood and made us free from the Law. In that way, the Law could not punish us. Christ did this by carrying the load and by being punished instead of us. It is written, "Anyone who hangs on a cross is hated and punished." Galatians 3:13 NLV

"I will not remember their sins and wrong-doings anymore." Hebrews 10:17 NLV

Let us keep looking to Jesus. Our faith comes from Him and He is the One Who makes it perfect. He did not give up when He had to suffer shame and die on a cross. He knew of the joy that would be His later. Now He is sitting at the right side of God. Hebrews 12:2 NLV

So we can say for sure, "The Lord is my Helper. I am not afraid of anything man can do to me." Hebrews 13:6 NLV

When God made a promise to Abraham, He made that promise in His own name because no one was greater. Hebrews 6:13 NLV

Each will be like a safe place from the wind, and a covering from the storm. Each will be like rivers of water in a dry country, and like the shadow of a large rock in a waste land. Isaiah 32:2 NLV

Do not fear, for I am with you. Do not be afraid, for I am your God. I will give you strength, and for sure I will help you. Yes, I will hold you up with My right hand that is right and good. Isaiah 41:10 NLV

The Spirit of the Lord God is on me, because the Lord has chosen me to bring good news to poor people. He has sent me to heal those with a sad heart. He has sent me to tell those who are being held and those in prison that they can go free. Isaiah 61:1 NLV

And they will call them "The holy people, the people who have been saved and set free by the Lord." And you will be called "A city looked for, a city that God has not forgotten." Isaiah 62:12 NLV

Whatever is good and perfect comes to us from God. He is the One Who made all light. He does not change. No shadow is made by His turning. James 1:17 NLV

There is no one like You, O Lord. You are great, and Your name is great in power. Jeremiah 10:6 NLV

The name of the Lord is a strong tower. The man who does what is right runs into it and is safe. Proverbs 18:10 NLV

He will not be afraid of bad news. His heart is strong because he trusts in the Lord. His heart will not be shaken. He will not be afraid and will watch those lose who fight against him. Psalm 112:7-8 NLV

He heals those who have a broken heart. He heals their sorrows. Psalm 147:3 NLV

I called to the Lord in my trouble. I cried to God for help. He heard my voice from His holy house. My cry for help came into His ears. Psalm 18:6 NLV

Those who are right with the Lord cry, and He hears them. And He takes them from all their troubles. The Lord is near to those who have a broken heart. And He saves those who are broken in spirit. Psalm 34:17-18 NLV

I will cry out and complain in the evening and morning and noon, and He will hear my voice. Psalm 55:17 NLV

I cried to Him with my mouth and praised Him with my tongue. Psalm 66:17 NLV

The Lord will not hear me if I hold on to sin in my heart. Psalm 66:18 NLV

FOREVER FRIENDS

But from there you will search again for the Lord your God. And if you search for him with all your heart and soul, you will find him. Deuteronomy 4:29 NLT

nothing in all creation will ever be able to separate us from the love of God that is revealed in Christ Jesus our Lord. Romans 8:39 NLT

"Yes, I am the vine; you are the branches. Those who remain in me, and I in them, will produce much fruit. For apart from me you can do nothing. John 15:5 NLT

The Lord isn't really being slow about his promise, as some people think. No, he is being patient for your sake. He does not want anyone to be destroyed, but wants everyone to repent. 2 Peter 3:9 NLT

I correct and discipline everyone I love. So be diligent and turn from your indifference. Revelation 3:19 NLT

And be sure of this: I am with you always, even to the end of the age." Matthew 28:20 NLT

I have written this to you who believe in the name of the Son of God, so that you may know you have eternal life. 1 John 5:13 NLT

And we know that the Son of God has come, and he has given us understanding so that we can know the true God. And now we live in fellowship with the true God because we live in fellowship with his Son, Jesus Christ. He is the only true God, and he is eternal life. 1 John 5:20 NLT

and await the mercy of our Lord Jesus Christ, who will bring you eternal life. In this way, you will keep yourselves safe in God's love. Jude 1:21 NLT

FREEDOM

If any of you lacks wisdom, you should ask God, who gives generously to all without finding fault, and it will be given to you. James 1:5 NIV

How much better to get wisdom than gold, to get insight rather than silver! Proverbs 16:16 NIV

When a mocker is punished, the simple gain wisdom; by paying attention to the wise they get knowledge. Proverbs 21:11 NIV

The beginning of wisdom is this: Get wisdom. Though it cost all you have, get understanding. Proverbs 4:7 NIV

But you are a chosen people, a royal priesthood, a holy nation, God's special possession, that you may declare the praises of him who called you out of darkness into his wonderful light. 1 Peter 2:9 NIV

Joshua went up to him and asked, "Are you for us or for our enemies?" "Neither," he replied, "but as commander of the army of the Lord I have now come." Joshua 5:13-14 NIV

The Lord thunders at the head of his army; his forces are beyond number, and mighty is the army that obeys his command. The day of the Lord is great; it is dreadful. Who can endure it? Joel 2:11 NIV

HE'S HERE

For this is what the high and exalted One says— he who lives forever, whose name is holy: "I live in a high and holy place, but also with the one who is contrite and lowly in spirit, to revive the spirit of the lowly and to revive the heart of the contrite. Isaiah 57:15 NIV

The Lord himself goes before you and will be with you; he will never leave you nor forsake you. Deuteronomy 31:8 NIV

Even though I walk through the darkest valley, I will fear no evil, for you are with me; your rod and your staff, they comfort me. Psalm 23:4 NIV

Have I not commanded you? Be strong and courageous. Do not be afraid; do not be discouraged, for the Lord your God will be with you wherever you go." Joshua 1:9 NIV

So do not fear, for I am with you Isaiah 41:10 NIV

But as for me, it is good to be near God. I have made the Sovereign Lord my refuge Psalm 73:28 NIV

I keep my eyes always on the Lord. With him at my right hand, I will not be shaken. Psalm 16:8 NIV

The Lord is close to the brokenhearted and saves those who are crushed in spirit. Psalm 34:18 NIV

Yet you are near, Lord, and all your commands are true. Psalm 119:151 NIV

The Lord is near to all who call on him, to all who call on him in truth. Psalm 145:18 NIV

"Am I only a God nearby," declares the Lord, "and not a God far away? Jeremiah 23:23 NIV

God did this so that they would seek him and perhaps reach out for him and find him, though he is not far from any one of us. Acts 17:27 NIV

But the priest said, "Let us inquire of God here." (for the law made nothing perfect), and a better hope is introduced, by which we draw near to God. Hebrews 7:19 NIV

Come near to God and he will come near to you. James 4:8 NIV

Whether you turn to the right or to the left, your ears will hear a voice behind you, saying, "This is the way; walk in it." Isaiah 30:21 NIV

Because of the Lord's great love we are not consumed, for his compassions never fail. They are new every morning; great is your faithfulness. Lamentations 3:22-23 NIV

He will cover you with his feathers, and under his wings you will find refuge; his faithfulness will be your shield and rampart. Psalm 91:4 NIV

Even to your old age and gray hairs I am he, I am he who will sustain you. I have made you and I will carry you; I will sustain you and I will rescue you. Isaiah 46:4 NIV

In all their distress he too was distressed, and the angel of his presence saved them. In his love and mercy he redeemed them; he lifted them up and carried them all the days of old. Isaiah 63:9 NIV

There you saw how the Lord your God carried you, as a father carries his son, all the way you went until you reached this place." Deuteronomy 1:31 NIV

For I am the Lord your God who takes hold of your right hand and says to you, Do not fear; I will help you. Isaiah 41:13 NIV

For he will command his angels concerning you to guard you in all your ways; Psalm 91:11 NIV

Lord, you have been our dwelling place throughout all generations. Psalm 90:1 NIV

Whoever dwells in the shelter of the Most High will rest in the shadow of the Almighty. Psalm 91:1 NIV

My people will live in peaceful dwelling places, in secure homes, in undisturbed places of rest. Isaiah 32:18 NIV

The eternal God is your refuge, and underneath are the everlasting arms. Deuteronomy 33:27 NIV

For in the day of trouble he will keep me safe in his dwelling; he will hide me in the shelter of his sacred tent and set me high upon a rock. Psalm 27:5 NIV

God is our refuge and strength, an ever-present help in trouble. Psalm 46:1 NIV

Let us then approach God's throne of grace with confidence, so that we may receive mercy and find grace to help us in our time of need. Hebrews 4:16 NIV

Trust in the Lord with all your heart and lean not on your own understanding; Proverbs 3:5 NIV

"The virgin will conceive and give birth to a son, and they will call him Immanuel" (which means "God with us"). Matthew 1:23 NIV

The virgin will conceive and give birth to a son, and will call him Immanuel. Isaiah 7:14 NIV

The Lord your God is with you, the Mighty Warrior who saves. He will take great delight in you; in his love he will no longer rebuke you, but will rejoice over you with singing." Zephaniah 3:17 NIV

Look to the Lord and his strength; seek his face always. 1 Chronicles 16:11 NIV

And so we know and rely on the love God has for us God is love. Whoever lives in love lives in God, and God in them. 1 John 4:16 NIV

For I am convinced that neither death nor life, neither angels nor demons, neither the present nor the future, nor any powers, neither height nor depth, nor anything else in all creation, will be able to separate us from the love of God that is in Christ Jesus our Lord. Romans 8:38-39 NIV

Where can I go from your Spirit? Where can I flee from your presence? If I go up to the heavens, you are there; if I make my bed in the depths, you are there. Psalm 139:8 NIV

See what great love the Father has lavished on us, that we should be called children of God! And that is what we are! The reason the world does not know us is that it did not know him. 1 John 3:1 NIV

He is before all things, and in him all things hold together. Colossians 1:17 NIV

one God and Father of all, who is over all and through all and in all. Ephesians 4:6 NIV

Jesus Christ is the same yesterday and today and forever. Hebrews 13:8 NIV

But whoever is united with the Lord is one with him in spirit. 1 Corinthians 6:17 NIV

This is how God showed his love among us: He sent his one and only Son into the world that we might live through him. 1 John 4:9 NIV

This is how we know that we live in him and he in us: He has given us of his Spirit. 1 John 4:13 NIV

"My prayer is not for them alone. I pray also for those who will believe in me through their message, that all of them may be one, Father, just as you are in me and I am in you. May they also be in us so that the world may believe that you have sent me. I have given them the glory that you gave me, that they may be one as we are one— I in them and you in me—so that they may be brought to complete unity. Then the world will know that you sent me and have loved them even as you have loved me. John 17:20-23 NIV

LOST AND FOUND

Do not be afraid or discouraged, for the Lord will personally go ahead of you. He will be with you; he will neither fail you nor abandon you." Deuteronomy 31:8 NLT

He will wipe every tear from their eyes, and there will be no more death or sorrow or crying or pain. All these things are gone forever." Revelation 21:4 NLT

I will rejoice over Jerusalem and delight in my people. And the sound of weeping and crying will be heard in it no more. Isaiah 65:19 NLT

O people of Zion, who live in Jerusalem, you will weep no more. He will be gracious if you ask for help. He will surely respond to the sound of your cries. Isaiah 30:19 NLT

He heals the brokenhearted and bandages their wounds. Psalm 147:3 NLT

For the Son of Man came to seek and save those who are lost." Luke 19:10 NLT

He did this to fulfill his own statement: "I did not lose a single one of those you have given me." John 18:9 NLT

"If a man has a hundred sheep and one of them gets lost, what will he do? Won't he leave the ninety-nine others in the wilderness and go to search for the one that is lost until he finds it? Luke 15:4 NLT

I will search for my lost ones who strayed away, and I will bring them safely home again. Ezekiel 34:16 NLT

If I go up to heaven, you are there; if I go down to the grave, you are there. Psalm 139:8 NLT

Who is like the Lord our God, the One who sits enthroned on high, who stoops down to look on the heavens and the earth? He raises the poor from the dust and lifts the needy from the ash heap Psalm 113:4-7 NIV

And he said to her, "Daughter, your faith has made you well. Go in peace. Your suffering is over." Mark 5:34 NLT

So I've learned from my experience that God protects the vulnerable. For I was broken and brought low, but he answered me and came to my rescue! Psalm 116:6 TPT

The Lord is slow to anger and filled with unfailing love Numbers 14:18 NLT

Listen to my voice in the morning, Lord. Each morning I bring my requests to you and wait expectantly. Psalm 5:3 NLT

"If you love me, obey my commandments. John 14:15 NLT

I waited patiently for the Lord to help me, and he turned to me and heard my cry. Psalm 40:1 NLT

You, too, must be patient. Take courage, for the coming of the Lord is near. James 5:8 NLT

What shall I repay to the Lord For all His benefits to me? Psalm 116:12 NASB

Jesus replied, "All who love me will do what I say. My Father will love them, and we will come and make our home with each of them. John 14:23 NLT

For even the Son of Man came not to be served but to serve others and to give his life as a ransom for many." Matthew 20:28 NLT

Loving God means keeping his commandments, and his commandments are not burdensome. 1 John 5:3 NLT

ONE DAY

If any of you lacks wisdom, you should ask God, who gives generously to all without finding fault, and it will be given to you. James 1:5 NIV

Teach us to number our days, that we may gain a heart of wisdom. Psalm 90:12 NIV

For wisdom will enter your heart, and knowledge will be pleasant to your soul. Proverbs 2:10 NIV

Blessed are those who find wisdom, those who gain understanding, Proverbs 3:13 NIV

For it is by grace you have been saved, through faith—and this is not from yourselves, it is the gift of God—

Ephesians 2:8 NIV

She is clothed with strength and dignity; she can laugh at the days to come. Proverbs 31:25 NIV

OPEN BOOK TESTS

I cried out to God for help; I cried out to God to hear me. When I was in distress, I sought the Lord; at night I stretched out untiring hands, and I would not be comforted.

I remembered you, God, and I groaned; I meditated, and my spirit grew faint. You kept my eyes from closing; I was too troubled to speak. I thought about the former days, the years of long ago; I remembered my songs in the night.

My heart meditated and my spirit asked: "Will the Lord reject forever? Will he never show his favor again? Has his unfailing love vanished forever? Has his promise failed for all time? Has God forgotten to be merciful? Has he in anger withheld his compassion?"

Then I thought, "To this I will appeal: the years when the Most High stretched out his right hand. I will remember the deeds of the Lord; yes, I will remember your miracles of long ago. I will consider all your works and meditate on all your mighty deeds."

Your ways, God, are holy. What god is as great as our God? You are the God who performs miracles; you display your power among the peoples. With your mighty arm you redeemed your people, the descendants of Jacob and Joseph. Psalm 77:1-15 NIV

PRAISE V. PAIN

---

pray for each other so that you may be healed. The prayer of a righteous person is powerful and effective. James 5:16 NIV

And the peace of God, which transcends all understanding, will guard your hearts and your minds in Christ Jesus. Philippians 4:7 NIV

Do not be anxious about anything, but in every situation, by prayer and petition, with thanksgiving, present your requests to God. Philippians 4:6 NIV

As you know, we count as blessed those who have persevered. You have heard of Job's perseverance and have seen what the Lord finally brought about. The Lord is full of compassion and mercy. James 5:11 NIV

This was to fulfill what was spoken through the prophet Isaiah: "He took up our infirmities and bore our diseases." Matthew 8:17 NIV

Jesus called his twelve disciples to him and gave them authority to drive out impure spirits and to heal every disease and sickness. Matthew 10:1 NIV

The Lord sustains them on their sickbed and restores them from their bed of illness. Psalm 41:3 NIV

You will not fear the terror of night, nor the arrow that flies by day Psalm 91:5 NIV

Is anyone among you in trouble? Let them pray. Is anyone happy? Let them sing songs of praise. Is anyone among you sick? Let them call the elders of the church to pray over them and anoint them with oil in the name of the Lord. And the prayer offered in faith will make the sick person well; the Lord will raise them up. If they have sinned, they will be forgiven. Therefore confess your sins to each other and pray for each other so that you may be healed. The prayer of a righteous person is powerful and effective. James 5:13-16 NIV

Be on your guard; stand firm in the faith; be courageous; be strong. 1 Corinthians 16:13 NIV

the people I formed for myself that they may proclaim my praise. Isaiah 43:21 NIV

Let everything that has breath praise the Lord. Praise the Lord. Psalm 150:6 NIV

"Do not fear, for I have redeemed you; I have summoned you by name; you are mine. When you pass through the waters, I will be with you; and when you pass through the rivers, they will not sweep over you. When you walk through the fire, you will not be burned; the flames will not set you ablaze. Since you are precious and honored in my sight, and because I love you, I will give people in exchange for you, nations in exchange for your life. Do not be afraid, for I am with you; Isaiah 43:1-2,4-5 NIV

SMILE

May the Lord smile on you and be gracious to you. May the Lord show you his favor and give you his peace. – Numbers 6:25-27 NLT

THE ART OF WAR

"My prayer is not for them alone. I also pray for those who will believe in me through their message, that all of them may be one, Father, just as you are in me and I am in you. May they also be in us so that the world may believe that you have sent me. I have given them the glory that you gave me, that they may be one as we are one—I in them and you in me—so that they may be brought to complete unity. Then the world will know that you sent me and have loved them even as you have loved me. John 17:20-23

THE LORD IS

In the beginning God created the heavens and the earth. Genesis 1:1 NIV

However, as it is written: "What no eye has seen, what no ear has heard, and what no human mind has conceived"— the things God has prepared for those who love him 1 Corinthians 2:9 NIV

Now to him who is able to do immeasurably more than all we ask or imagine, according to his power that is at work within us Ephesians 3:20 NIV

And God is able to bless you abundantly, so that in all things at all times, having all that you need, you will abound in every good work. 2 Corinthians 9:8 NIV

Therefore he is able to save completely those who come to God through him, because he always lives to intercede for them. Hebrews 7:25 NIV

but in these last days he has spoken to us by his Son, whom he appointed heir of all things, and through whom also he made the universe. Hebrews 1:2 NIV

She will give birth to a son, and you are to give him the name Jesus, because he will save his people from their sins." Matthew 1:21 NIV

He is not here; he has risen, just as he said. Come and see the place where he lay. Matthew 28:6 NIV

For God so loved the world that he gave his one and only Son, that whoever believes in him shall not perish but have eternal life. John 3:16 NIV

Then the Lord God formed a man from the dust of the ground and breathed into his nostrils the breath of life, and the man became a living being. Genesis 2:7 NIV

If you belong to Christ, then you are Abraham's seed, and heirs according to the promise. Galatians 3:29 NIV

He said to them, "Go into all the world and preach the gospel to all creation. Mark 16:15 NIV

"Meaningless! Meaningless!" says the Teacher. "Utterly meaningless! Everything is meaningless." Ecclesiastes 1:2 NIV

The fear of the Lord is the beginning of knowledge, but fools despise wisdom and instruction. Proverbs 1:7 NIV

The fear of the Lord is the beginning of wisdom, and knowledge of the Holy One is understanding. Proverbs 9:10 NIV

For the word of God is alive and active. Sharper than any double-edged sword, it penetrates even to dividing soul and spirit, joints and marrow; it judges the thoughts and attitudes of the heart. Hebrews 4:12 NIV

Hold on to instruction, do not let it go guard it well, for it is your life. Proverbs 4:13 NIV

All Scripture is God-breathed and is useful for teaching, rebuking, correcting and training in righteousness, so that the servant of God may be thoroughly equipped for every good work. 2 Timothy 3:16-17 NIV

WALK WITH HIM

Grace, mercy and peace from God the Father and from Jesus Christ, the Father's Son, will be with us in truth and love. 2 John 1:3 NIV

Let us then approach God's throne of grace with confidence, so that we may receive mercy and find grace to help us in our time of need. Hebrews 4:16 NIV

We are convinced that everyone fathered by God does not make sinning a way of life, because the Son of God protects the child of God, and the Evil One cannot touch him. 1 John 5:18 TPT

Then Jesus declared, "I am the bread of life. Whoever comes to me will never go hungry, and whoever believes in me will never be thirsty. John 6:35 NIV

To the thirsty I will give water without cost from the spring of the water of life. Revelation 21:6 NIV

Let the one who is thirsty come; and let the one who wishes take the free gift of the water of life. Revelation 22:17 NIV

For whoever wants to save their life will lose it, but whoever loses their life for me will save it. Luke 9:24 NIV

Don't you know that you yourselves are God's temple and that God's Spirit dwells in your midst? 1 Corinthians 3:16 NIV

But even before I was born, God chose me and called me by his marvelous grace. Then it pleased him

Galatians 1:15 NLT

The twelve gates were made of pearls—each gate from a single pearl! And the main street was pure gold, as clear as glass. Revelation 21:21 NLT

You watched me as I was being formed in utter seclusion, as I was woven together in the dark of the womb. You saw me before I was born. Every day of my life was recorded in your book. Every moment was laid out before a single day had passed. Psalm 139:13-16 NLT

The one who does what is sinful is of the devil, because the devil has been sinning from the beginning. The reason the Son of God appeared was to destroy the devil's work. 1 John 3:8 NIV

"Before I formed you in the womb I knew you, before you were born I set you apart; I appointed you as a prophet to the nations." Jeremiah 1:5 NIV

My child, never forget the things I have taught you. Store my commands in your heart. Proverbs 3:1 NLT

The Lord says, "I will rescue those who love me. I will protect those who trust in my name. Psalm 91:14 NLT

The Spirit alone gives eternal life. Human effort accomplishes nothing. And the very words I have spoken to you are spirit and life. John 6:63 NLT

God has now revealed to us his mysterious will regarding Christ—which is to fulfill his own good plan.

Ephesians 1:9 NLT

No, the wisdom we speak of is the mystery of God—his plan that was previously hidden, even though he made it for our ultimate glory before the world began. 1 Corinthians 2:7 NLT

Because of the joy awaiting him, he endured the cross, disregarding its shame. Now he is seated in the place of honor beside God's throne. Hebrews 12:2 NLT

Carrying the cross by himself, he went to the place called Place of the Skull John 19:17 NLT

And they spit on him and grabbed the stick and struck him on the head with it. Matthew 27:30 NLT

They wove thorn branches into a crown and put it on his head, and they placed a reed stick in his right hand as a scepter. Matthew 27:29 NLT

The eternal God is your refuge, and his everlasting arms are under you. Deuteronomy 33:27-28 NLT

So God created human beings in his own image. In the image of God he created them; male and female he created them. Genesis 1:27 NLT

The thief's purpose is to steal and kill and destroy. My purpose is to give them a rich and satisfying life. John 10:10 NLT

Since we have been united with him in his death, we will also be raised to life as he was. Romans 6:5 NLT

We are made right with God by placing our faith in Jesus Christ. And this is true for everyone who believes, no matter who we are. Romans 3:22 NLT

Therefore, since we have been made right in God's sight by faith, we have peace with God because of what Jesus Christ our Lord has done for us. Romans 5:1 NLT

But God showed his great love for us by sending Christ to die for us while we were still sinners. And since we have been made right in God's sight by the blood of Christ, he will certainly save us from God's condemnation. For since our friendship with God was restored by the death of his Son while we were still his enemies, we will certainly be saved through the life of his Son. Romans 5:8-10 NLT

Christ's one act of righteousness brings a right relationship with God and new life for everyone. Because one person disobeyed God, many became sinners. But because one other person obeyed God, many will be made righteous. Romans 5:18-19 NLT

When Jesus heard this, he said, "Healthy people don't need a doctor—sick people do." Matthew 9:12 NLT

For I have come to call not those who think they are righteous, but those who know they are sinners." Matthew 9:13 NLT

And this is my covenant with them, that I will take away their sins." Romans 11:27 NLT

Just as you who were at one time disobedient to God have now received mercy as a result of their disobedience Romans 11:30 NIV

For the Son of Man came to seek and to save the lost." Luke 19:9-10 NIV

With this in mind, we constantly pray for you, that our God may make you worthy of his calling, and that by his power he may bring to fruition your every desire for goodness and your every deed prompted by faith. 2 Thessalonians 1:11 NIV

Now the earth was formless and empty, darkness was over the surface of the deep, and the Spirit of God was hovering over the waters. Genesis 1:2 NIV

If we confess our sins, he is faithful and just and will forgive us our sins and purify us from all unrighteousness. 1 John 1:9 NIV

Repent, then, and turn to God, so that your sins may be wiped out, that times of refreshing may come from the Lord Acts 3:19 NIV

For I will forgive their wickedness and will remember their sins no more." Hebrews 8:12 NIV

God is faithful, who has called you into fellowship with his Son, Jesus Christ our Lord. 1 Corinthians 1:9 NIV

Let your eyes look straight ahead; fix your gaze directly before you. Give careful thought to the paths for your feet and be steadfast in all your ways. Do not turn to the right or the left; keep your foot from evil. Proverbs 4:24-27 NIV

So we fix our eyes not on what is seen, but on what is unseen, since what is seen is temporary, but what is unseen is eternal. 2 Corinthians 4:18 NIV

Therefore, holy brothers and sisters, who share in the heavenly calling, fix your thoughts on Jesus, whom we acknowledge as our apostle and high priest. Hebrews 3:1 NIV

Jesus answered, "I am the way and the truth and the life. No one comes to the Father except through me. John 14:6 NIV

Surely I was sinful at birth, sinful from the time my mother conceived me. Psalm 51:5 NIV

Even from birth the wicked go astray; from the womb they are wayward Psalm 58:3 NIV

Indeed, there is no one on earth who is righteous, no one who does what is right and never sins. Ecclesiastes 7:20 NIV

Jesus replied, "Very truly I tell you, no one can see the kingdom of God unless they are born again." John 3:3 NIV

If you declare with your mouth, "Jesus is Lord," and believe in your heart that God raised him from the dead, you will be saved. For it is with your heart that you believe and are justified, and it is with your mouth that you profess your faith and are saved. As Scripture says, "Anyone who believes in him will never be put to shame." …the same Lord is Lord of all and richly blesses all who call on him, for, "Everyone who calls on the name of the Lord will be saved." How, then, can they call on the one they have not believed in? And how can they believe in the one of whom they have not heard? And how can they hear without someone preaching to them? And how can anyone preach unless they are sent? As it is written: "How beautiful are the feet of those who bring good news!" … Consequently, faith comes from hearing the message, and the message is heard through the word about Christ. Romans 10:9-17 NIV

Love is patient, love is kind. It does not envy, it does not boast, it is not proud. It does not dishonor others, it is not self-seeking, it is not easily angered, it keeps no record of wrongs. Love does not delight in evil but rejoices with the truth. It always protects, always trusts, always hopes, always perseveres. 1 Corinthians 13:4-7 NIV

See what great love the Father has lavished on us, that we should be called children of God! And that is what we are! The reason the world does not know us is that it did not know him. Dear friends, now we are children of God, and what we will be has not yet been made known. But we know that when Christ appears, we shall be like him, for we shall see him as he is. All who have this hope in him purify themselves, just as he is pure. Everyone who sins breaks the law; in fact, sin is lawlessness. But you know that he appeared so that he might take away our sins. And in him is no sin. No one who lives in him keeps on sinning. No one who continues to sin has either seen him or known him. Dear children, do not let anyone lead you astray. The one who does what is right is righteous, just as he is righteous. 1 John 3:1-7 NIV

REFLECTIONS

evenifmemoir.com

REFLECTIONS

evenifmemoir.com

REFLECTIONS

REFLECTIONS

evenifmemoir.com

ABOUT THE AUTHOR

Hadiyah Bobbitt's poetic prowess began when penning her first poem at the age of seven. Her work is in styles and genres as eclectic as her personality. She writes with humor and candor on the spoils of wars won with an empowered posture of faith and tenacity in life's inevitable tribulation.

A Brooklyn-Girl dubbed a soldier-in-stilettos for her warrior spirit—in her debut publication, she gives a preview of a life that underscores survival is situational—resilience is a lifestyle.

Losing her sister to suicide fuels a passionate drive to touch the hearts and minds of those suffering in silence. She uses her writing as an instrument of healing, with a deep desire to reach the world with words that soothe the weariest souls.

In her youth, Hadiyah was an active spoken word artist. She has also had roles in television, film, voice acting, and supporting roles performing in the music industry.

In her career of more than 15 years, Hadiyah is a risk management professional with extensive experience in the banking industry.

An unfettered imagination and an insatiable wanderlust often take her across the globe, zip-lining through rainforests in Central America one month and chasing waterfalls and Northern Lights in Nordic Countries in the next.

When home in New York, her heart's resting place is serving in her church, Christian Cultural Center led by Pastors Dr. A. R. Bernard and Dr. Karen Bernard in Brooklyn, New York, and with her spiritual sisters and extended family.

EVEN IF I GIVE MY LIFE AS A GIFT ON THE ALTAR TO GOD FOR YOU, I AM GLAD AND SHARE THIS JOY WITH YOU.

PHILIPPIANS 2:17 NLV

FOR LIVE SPOKEN WORD PERFORMANCES VISIT

evenifmemoir.com/sayword

VISIT THE ONLINE STORE FOR ADDITIONAL BOOKS, MEMOIR MERCH, AND MORE.

Made in the USA
Middletown, DE
10 January 2022